Uncommon Views of Common Verses

John H. Hill

Unless otherwise indicated, Bible quotations are taken from the Authorized Version (KJV) of the Bible (Public Domain) and from the author's personal translations of the Holy Scriptures.

Uncommon Views of Common Verses

Published by John H. Hill Publishing

1501 Central Avenue

Summerville, SC 29483

ISBN 978-1-257-09038-9

Dedication

To my father, William Hundley Hill, who taught me as a child to love his Savior and God's Word. Although he made no great impression far beyond the central parts of North Carolina, he made a deep and abiding impression on all who knew him. His spirit was soft and gentle – drawing people to his Lord through his consistent and faithful daily living.

Dad met his Lord in person on January 7, 1999. Heaven became sweeter for me on that day, and I look forward to seeing him at the feet of Jesus, near the River of Life.

Acknowledgments

These short studies have been exciting for me as I worked through verses, sought advice, and put together these thoughts. In order to have a "readable" text that made sense – hoping and praying that the over-looked would not fade into obscurity, I engaged the students of my Bible class at Ferndale Baptist School in North Charleston, SC. Many thanks go to the following students, who read, marked with red ink, and gave verbal feedback. Their editing helped insure the devotionals were readable. Matt Ashley, Robert Barrs, Knysna Broom, Brandon Chapman, Coleen Cobb, Chris Doss, Franklin Duberry, Jacob Gruber, Kaylee Hill, T.A. Horn, Kaytlyn Jennings, Shelby Jennings, Kalyn Knupp, Devin Muffley, Victoria Murray, Adam Nelson, Joel Price, Dillon Ridenour, Abbie Rysta, Christian Sloane, Holly Tyrpak, and Adam Williams.

A special thanks to Sarah Crawford, who, although a former student, volunteered her time to read and correct several articles for me. Thank you, Sarah.

April Howze, whom I have known since she was a baby, did the final editing. Mother, youth pastor's wife, and otherwise extremely busy; she offered her expertise with the English language.

Finally, to my wife (Nancy) and children (Lindy and Kaylee), many thanks for giving me "space" in which to do my work. The Bible has said it best, *"Whoso findeth a wife findeth a good thing, and obtaineth favor of the Lord,"* (Proverbs 18.22) and *"Lo, children are a heritage of the LORD: and the fruit of the womb is his reward."* (Psalm 127.3) I am a man truly blessed.

Forward

While reading through God's Word, quite often I come across verses or passages that greatly intrigue me because of a special poetic "feel" or simply because they immediately create curiosity in my mind. When that happens, I want to know what others (more learned than myself) have written as explanations. It is not uncommon to realize that, many times, writers skip over difficult or obscure passages or give explanations that seem to satisfy little (maybe they have the same difficulties as the rest of us). I, in no means, am disparaging great writers, either past or present, but am simply saying that my curiosity and desire to know God and His Word sometimes overwhelms me.

Uncommon Views of Common Verses looks at verses, many times overlooked, and offers explanations, exegeses, and applications for the believer who loves his Lord. Every attempt has been made to be true to God's Word because it alone is the *"power of God unto salvation." (Romans 1.16)* Taking into consideration the original languages, context, and culture, I have written (keeping in mind that Scripture places the Lord Jesus Christ central in every page) in simple language some easy-to-understand, devotional articles for your consideration. Some may surprise you; others may shock you, but I trust all will be a blessing to you as you study God's Word. *(II Timothy 3.16, 17)*

Table of Contents

The Kingdom or Paradise, Luke 23.42, 43

"And he said unto Jesus, Lord, remember me when thou comest into thy kingdom. And Jesus said unto him, Verily I say unto thee, To day shalt thou be with me in paradise." (Luke 23:43)

Quite often in Scripture direct questions seem to be answered in not so direct manners. Such is the case in the passage before us.

While on the cross, after some time of great suffering, one of the two thieves who was crucified beside our Lord, turned to Him and asked to be remembered when He came into His kingdom. Jesus, in reply, told the repentant thief that they would be together that same day in Paradise. What is interesting in this exchange is that the thief asked for a kingdom and Jesus offered paradise.

The word used for Kingdom is from the Greek word ***basilieia*** and carries the idea of a rule or reign. It should not be, according to Thayer, confused with an actual kingdom, but rather the right of authority to rule over the kingdom. In essence, the thief was asking Jesus to remember him when Jesus took His rightful place of authority in His kingdom.

On the other hand, the word ***paradise*** is somewhat of a transliteration rather than a translation. It is of a Persian origin and was used to denote a *grand enclosure, preserve, hunting grounds, and a well-watered shady park.* Often this "paradise" would be closely attached to a large dwelling or mansion. It could be a basis for the idea of a "happy hunting ground."

Without getting into a theological discussion about the differences or similarities in the statements "Kingdom of heaven" and "Kingdom of God," it would appear that the dying criminal understood the part about repentance and submission to God's authority. He not only called Jesus Lord, but he also acknowledged Jesus' right to rule.

Although it took a cross with tremendous pain, the thief was brought face-to-face with his need of a Righteous Leader. What is fascinating about his faith is that he asked this of Jesus while Jesus was in no earthly position to deliver anyone from anything. This was true faith in the unseen and the apparent unlikely; however, the thief believed in Jesus' authority and right to rule. Remember the words of our Lord to Thomas, "Blessed are they that have not seen, and yet have believed" (*John 20.29*).

When Jesus answered the thief, He did so in a manner that is characteristic of our Lord. The thief simply asked to be remembered. Our Lord offered him a place of abundance and pure delight.

Many times this paradise was attached to a large manor house and seems to be suggestive of the "mansions" of *John 14* where Christ Jesus explains that there are in His Father's house many dwelling places. The saved will one day inherit, not only a place of residence in the Father's house, but will also be allowed access to Paradise because it is a part of the Father's house. We will be allowed freedom to come and go – to go in and out and find pasture. Our's will be the blessings of our Lord.

An almost overlooked application is found in the fact that the things for which we long and seek in no way compare to what God offers. We ask for food, He offers a feast. We ask for things, He offers pleasures for evermore. We ask for companionship, He offers everlasting love. We ask for money to pay the bills, He paves His streets with gold.

In our finite and feeble minds, we have no idea of the greatness of our God. Because of that, we can trust Him to both know what is best for us and to do what is best for us in every situation of life. He is a great God who loves His children. (*Ephesians 3.20; I Corinthians 2.9*)

The Nearest Kinsman, Ruth 4.1

"Then went Boaz up to the gate, and sat him down there: and, behold, the kinsman of whom Boaz spake came by; unto whom he said, Ho, such a one! turn aside, sit down here. And he turned aside, and sat down." (Ruth 4.1)

The book of Ruth puts forth an almost fairy tale-like story of a young lady who was widowed and without hope (except for her mother-in-law) and in a foreign country.

It seems that she had no friends to speak of because even her sister-in-law (also widowed) turned back home when Naomi (the mother-in-law) urged her to do so. Now Ruth was going to a strange land to live with strange people who served a different God solely because of her good relationship with Naomi. Naomi, too, was without hope because her husband had died, their substance was gone due to a famine, and they had been away from God and His people for many years.

After having returned to Naomi's homeland, the two ladies began setting up house-keeping. One of the immediate tasks was to gather food – which Ruth did heartily and readily.

Ruth proved herself to be godly and industrious in her attitude and work ethics. As a result she was noticed by one of the very important land owners of the area – Boaz. Boaz happened to be her near-kinsman. That meant that he was in a position to redeem her and her land for the proper price.

The redemption was a matter of restoring people, land, and possessions to the original owner because all of it had been "loaned" to them by God and was to never leave their possession. By going to the far country, Naomi's family had relinquished their God-given rights to the land, and therefore was at the mercy of redeemers.

It is not my intent to minimize the story itself, but most know it already. There is, however, a story lesser told that concerns the right to redemption and approach to the redeemer.

When Ruth made her approach, Boaz commended her for her actions by pointing out that she had not gone after other, younger men but that she sought the better way. This showed that she was interested in preserving for Naomi what should remain as family possessions. Ruth sought what was right rather than what was comfortable.

Through the story, however, God shows that when you do right (by accepting His provision for salvation), He will make you accepted in the beloved – a place of comfort and happiness.

The thought that seemed to spring from the pages concerns the redeemer and the "*nearest*" redeemer. It is readily accepted that Boaz is a type of the kinsman Redeemer (Christ) and that Ruth is a type of the Church. But the picture is far more telling than just that.

The question arises concerning this "*nearest*" kinsman. Had Ruth not approached Boaz, all the possessions, and Ruth herself, would have been subject to the other kinsman. He would have used her inheritance as his own and could have, and most probably would have, treated Ruth as a slave. That can be seen in the fact that he did not wish to redeem her – only her land.

It seems that the nearest kinsman should represent the god of this world – Satan (*John 8.44*). As the nearest kinsman and rightful owner of this world and all that is in it by virtue of the original ceding over to him by Adam, legally and ethically he controls the power and authority of this world. He is able to do as he wishes with the property and assets, and enslave all who are children of the world.

When Jesus died on the cross, He paid the redemption price for the entire world. There is now none who are enslaved by reason of a lack of funds. Jesus' blood accomplished "funds" that could satisfy the cost for the most heinous of sins and sinners. There is enough payment to satisfy any and all debts that are owed.

On the cross, in the dark hours, our Lord faced Satan, won the victory, and paid the price for sin. Many are still in the far country experiencing want because of famine. Some have come home to familiar surroundings but are still without freedom and happiness because they continue to look to the god of this world for the world's blessings.

I trust that you will be one who will seek the One who is the true, loving Redeemer. Jesus Christ will redeem your soul from hell, and He will also give to you blessings of family and fellowship that the world cannot offer.

The choice is to be a slave to this world's god or to be free and redeemed by the precious Lamb of God.

The Helmet of Salvation, Ephesians 6.17

"And take the helmet of salvation, and the sword of the Spirit, which is the word of God:" (Ephesians 6.17)

When reading this passage concerning spiritual warfare and the donning of armor for protection, we become excited by the fact that God has called us to be a part of the fray and also has given us preparation for protection, battle, and victory. Each piece of armor is a vital part of our equipment.

In all, Paul lists six pieces that make up our full complement for both defense and offense so that we can stand (*Ephesians 6.14*). The first piece has been considered by most to be a defensive part of the armor because having a *"girdle"* or *"belt"* to maintain control of the robes while running does not at first seem to be anything offensive. However, it is necessary that one have freedom of movement in order to attack. This represents truth. By being clean of falseness, misinformation, or even lies, the soldier can bravely go into the spiritual battle without fear of contradiction.

The second piece of armor is called the *"breastplate of righteousness."* The breastplate will cover any vital organ so the soldier cannot be slain from a wound to the chest – and specifically to the heart. The Bible clearly tells us to keep our heart.

The third piece to the armor is a pair of proper *"shoes."* In any contest, or in everyday life, proper shoes are essential. No one would try to run a race in hip waders nor would anyone go trout fishing in track shoes. The Roman soldiers were able to gain a tremendous advantage over their enemies by wearing shoes with cleats to help keep their feet from slipping. Likewise the Christian soldier must prepare himself with the Gospel of Peace so that his feet will not slip as he contends for the faith.

Concerning the *"shield,"* the Bible uses the word that speaks of a large shield. In the soldier's arsenal, he had at his disposal a shield behind which he could crouch and be completely hidden from the enemy's assault. No matter how many spears or fiery projectiles were sent, they would all be rendered impotent because of the shield. Sometimes, when reason fails, faith is victorious because we look not at earthly things, but toward God Who is in all and yet above all. Faith in our precious Savior will calm all the storms and dissuade all arguments. *"Looking unto Jesus, the author and finisher of our faith..." (Hebrews 12.2a)*.

The fact that the *"helmet of salvation"* is listed fifth in this catalog has caused some to wonder why. This should not bring us great alarm because, since the Epistle to the Ephesians was written to believers (*Ephesians 1.1*), it stands to reason that salvation in each one is assumed. Hence, this part would not pertain to the individual's salvation from sin and to the Savior through belief in Christ's shed blood. It must refer to something after salvation which becomes a part of the believer's defense. But what?

A helmet in this passage comes from a word that literally means to encircle the head. Salvation, basically, means to be delivered from something and in this case, from the attacks of the enemy. So then, the soldier must enclose his head with deliverance from Christ through the Word. In essence, every thought must be brought into captivity and sifted through a fine scrutiny of the Word of God. Every thought, attitude, and action should be examined as it is related to our salvation. No action should pass the mental test unless it has passed the test of conformity to our salvation in Christ. So then, the helmet protects our thought processes making certain that what we think is in line with our Savior's will.

In the defensive position for the Christian soldier, only one piece of equipment stands out as distinctively offensive – the *"Sword of the Spirit,"* which is the Word of God. Lest we get too carried away by the tremendous power of God's Word, we should take a moment to reflect on the fact that our speech, attitudes, and actions must be calculated and calibrated according to the *"helmet of salvation."* The Sword cannot properly be wielded until the Christian's thought process is in line with the Spirit of God.

Quite often we need to remind ourselves to have our brain running before putting our mouth in gear. Many have fallen in battle, even though victory was attainable, because they were wielding their own sword and not the *"Sword of the Spirit."* Spiritual victories are won without might and without power, but not without God's Spirit.

We should pray earnestly that the words of our mouths and the meditations of our hearts are acceptable to God, thereby being a strong force in showing others the way to victory in Christ (*Psalm 19.14*).

Pitch and More Pitch, Genesis 6.14

"There were giants in the earth in those days; and also after that, when the sons of God came in unto the daughters of men, and they bare *children* to them, the same *became* mighty men which *were* of old, men of renown."

(Genesis 6.14)

Often when reading the Bible, my attention is arrested by phrases that seem to be obscure or ones that do not seem to have an easy English understanding. In *Genesis 6.14* there is such a phrase that has caught my attention for several years as a rather "sing-songy" poetic phrase that just sounds good when it rolls off my lips. The phrase *"pitch it within and without with pitch"* caught my attention.

When looking a little beyond the obvious, I came to the conclusion that there is a wealth of blessing to be gained from this one small phrase. In order to have this blessing, we must go to the original language and see what is there.

The obvious lessons concerning the Ark deal with the fact that God cares for those who love and obey Him. Beyond that, Noah and his family show how godly people can, and must, stand for God in their evil generations. Prophetically, Noah pictures God's people (specifically the Jewish nation) who will be preserved to inhabit the Millennial Kingdom after suffering great tribulation.

What is not openly seen is the manner in which God provides. When going through a storm in life, it seems that the anticipation of the coming problem is always worse than the situation itself. During each crisis for a believer, there is a peace in knowing we are not alone. That is the picture given through the Ark.

This phrase suggests volumes that offer aid to an aching heart and soul. There is a definite and severe difference between those who are redeemed and those who are not. The Ark graphically illustrates this by the fact that some are outside while others are inside. The doorway obviously pictures admittance by God alone – through Christ.

Two different, but closely related Hebrew words are translated into our English word **pitch**. The first **pitch** is the Hebrew word **kapar** which means *"to cover, to forgive, to expiate, and to reconcile"* and generally, throughout Scripture is translated as *"atonement."* The other word is **koper** and means *"ransom or bribe."*

The word that indicates atonement means more than a mere covering. In the Ark, this atonement sealed the inside of the structure. That speaks of safety and security. On the outside, was the ransom paid in order for someone to be admitted. So then, the Ark was sealed inside and out by the atonement and ransom respectively. The ransom was paid and admittance gained through the Door, and only the Door, because there was no other way to enter. Once inside and the Door shut, there was no way out until the storm was over and God opened the Door.

That is not the end of the story. The word **without** is a simple word meaning something or someone who is not on the inside. How terribly obvious. What is significant is the word **within**. It means *"house, home, household, palace, temple, and family."* A suggested application is a sanctuary – a place where someone feels comfortable, safe, and at ease.

All around the Ark, the world was being destroyed by the greatest catastrophe ever; yet, inside the Ark, Noah and his family found peace and comfort – safety and rest. Inside the sanctuary all were comfortable in their *"rooms"* which, literally translated, means *"nests"* or *"lairs."*

The person who is *in* Christ finds that he has an ever present Savior Who brings peace and security. When a person trusts Christ as Savior, He not only saves, but He also is a close personal Friend Who cares for the weary and comforts the troubled. Even though it may seem that the entire world is falling apart, in Christ there is safety.

Chains of Darkness, Jude 1.6

"And the angels which kept not their first estate, but left their own habitation, he hath reserved in everlasting chains under darkness unto the judgment of the great day." (Jude 1.6)

An often misunderstood and overlooked verse is *Jude 1.6*. Bible students, for years, have struggled with the meaning and have assigned various (and sometimes fanciful) interpretations to it.

It would seem that the most common interpretation of *Jude 1.6*, which speaks of angels being under chains of darkness, is that these angels were a part of an original rebellion against God. In that rebellion, Satan left his intended position of honor as the anointed cherub and there were some angels in the original, angelic rebellion that were so diabolical that God incarcerated them in a place of darkness. Some of these may, according to this interpretation, be the ones who are released from the River Euphrates during the Great Tribulation Period.

From that interpretation, those fallen angels must be divided into at least two categories. The first are those who are still loose on the earth and have opportunity to create havoc for Christians. The other group includes those that were so bad that God has already relegated them to hell which is, essentially, outer darkness.

A major problem in following that line of reasoning is that since Satan must be the worst of the bad, he should have been the first one to be sent to outer darkness. He should be suffering that predicament. Since it is obvious he is not now bound (*I Peter 5.8*), one holding to the previous conclusion must give thought concerning how bad those in chains really are if they are indeed worse than Satan. The question, "Why would God show favoritism to Satan over some of Satan's demons?" and "How can we reconcile the fact that there still seems to be so much evil in the world?"

Since man is the crown of creation, and the object of God's love; and, since the angels were created for mankind to be ministering spirits (*Hebrews 1.14*); leaving their first estate (primary function) would result in their dismissal from their privileged position. The relationship God has with the angels is quite different from that with humanity. The angels are servants who rush to please their Creator; but when they rebel, they are cast out of their privileged place. Since they have no Redeemer, they are relegated to a lost condition with no hope of salvation. That place, then, is one of spiritual darkness (*Acts 26.18; Romans 2.19; II Peter 2.4*).

When man first sinned against God, God already had in place a plan for his restoration and redemption (*Revelation 13.8*) – the blood of the Lamb of God. When the angels sinned against God and chose to decline their proper place of service to God and mankind, there was no plan for restoration. The angels who left their first estate were destined for hell, which was originally prepared for the devil and his angels (*Matthew 25.41*).

The darkness in *Jude 1.6* refers to a spiritual darkness and suggests a *mist* or *cloud*. Although the fallen angels can see and hear everything that pertains to the Bible and God, their minds have been clouded to God's goodness because they lack opportunity for salvation. Remember, Paul recorded that *"had they known they would not have crucified the Lord of Glory" (I Corinthians 2.8)*. This spiritual darkness under which they operate now will continue until they stand before the judgment of God. According to *Revelation 20*, Satan will be physically bound, but now he is not. He and those who follow him are reserved in chains under darkness until they will be judged by the Almighty God for their rebellious deeds.

Hair – the Long and Short of It, I Corinthians 11.1-15

"Doth not even nature itself teach you, that, if a man have long hair, it is a shame unto him? But if a woman have long hair, it is a glory to her: for *her* hair is given her for a covering." (I Corinthians 11.14, 15)

Growing up in the 60s, in rural North Carolina, the shaggy haired look caught on rather slowly (as did the Beatles) – but catch on it did. As a result, our pastor (and seemingly every evangelist who came through) would preach hard against long hair on men. After all, according to the Scriptures, it was a shame and disgrace for men to have long hair.

Many a young lad (myself included) would ask the question, "How long is long?" There were a variety of answers given that seemed to make sense to the one giving the answer. The answer that made the most sense to me was when my father (a godly man) told me to get a haircut, so I got a haircut. On only one occasion, it obviously was not to his standard so he loaded me in his truck and took me back. Dad set the standard at our house. The problem was that one day, as I grew up; I left home, went to college, and married. So what is my standard?

In our efforts to bolster our point, the young men would cite the fact that God had ordered Samson to never cut his hair. Within the last few years, one gentleman (now with our Lord) said that he would never allow a woman to cut his hair (even though his daughter owned a hair salon) because if a woman cut his hair he would lose his strength like Samson did. He may have spoken in jest or having forgotten that Delilah was not the one who cut Samson's hair, but she called in barbers to do the work. It seems that almost everyone has an opinion, or at least a comment, about hair. To further exacerbate a young mind was the lack of mention about a woman's hair. Certainly if a man should have short hair, the woman should have long hair.

The point is that most seemed to miss the point by treating a symptom rather than the real issue. Paul makes the issue quite clear to any who will read without preconceived ideas. Since Paul is writing about relationships and chains of command, the discussion concerning hair must be considered in that context.

Paul's opening statement in verse one sets the stage for this chain of authority. In essence, Paul says for the Corinthians to follow (be an imitator of) him just as he is an imitator of Christ. He then proceeds to explain the order of authority.

Men in the church should take the lead. This alone, in modern churches, is not what many want to hear but the fact remains – men should take the lead. Short hair on men symbolizes the fact that there should be no obstacles between man and God – nothing shrouding man's direct approach to and access to the Father.

Since God has placed man in this position as spiritual leader, he must maintain open communications with God in order to so pattern his life. The short hair is simply an outward symbol of his commitment to his Savior. To cover his head with long hair shows that he is not willing to take the position that God has entrusted to him but prefers a position of secondary approach.

The woman's responsibility is ultimately to her Savior, but Paul teaches that without order, God will not be honored. As a matter of fact, it was disorder and lack of a proper understanding that led to problems in the Garden of Eden.

In order for God to be honored, order must prevail; and since God has placed the man directly responsible to Him and directly under His authority in the home and church, the woman should show her submission to her husband and thereby honor God. Having long hair is an outward symbol that she is submissive to her husband, but ultimately submissive to God. To not be submissive to her husband or to have shortly cropped hair shows outwardly her aversion to being godly.

Does that mean that every man with long hair and every woman with short hair is barred from approach to God? No, but it does seem to indicate that some take the way of worldly styles rather than God-given styles. The argument that short hair is easier to manage skirts the real issue because it is the same argument the world uses. Maybe it does take time to show our submission to our Master, but that is an outward sign of our inward love.

The woman's example to follow is that of the angels in heaven who willingly cover themselves when in the presence of God (*Isaiah 6.2*). The angels take no liberties when in God's presence. They willingly, yea, joyfully submit to their holy God.

It behooves every believer to be submissive to the proper authority (whether earthly rulers or God Himself) so that the name of our precious Savior may be exalted. Let us lift up His name by our actions, attitudes, and appearances. After all, this is not about a life of ease, but a life of love for Christ.

The Amplified Bible translates *I Corinthians 11.10* as follows: *"Therefore she should {be subject to his authority and should} have a covering on her head {as a token, a symbol, of her submission to authority, that she may show reverence as do} the angels {and not displease them}."* (Lockman Foundation. La Habra, CA, 1987.)

Owe No Man Anything, Romans 13.8

"Owe no man any thing, but to love one another: for he that loveth another hath fulfilled the law." (Romans 13.8)

With credit cards and borrowed money easily obtainable, it would seem that this part of Scripture may be questioned as to its modern applications. At one time, because of one's ability to deduct certain amounts of interest from income taxes, owing money seemed to be better than not owing. Once, when I was young, a fellow church-member told me flatly that I needed to take on some debt in order to establish credit. If I did not, I would get nowhere in the world.

That, however, did not agree with what I had been taught from Scripture. When in college, one professor suggested that this needed to be applied only when payments on loans were overdue. His suggestion was that no one should allow themselves to get behind.

Others would say that this verse tells the Christian that it is never right to borrow money of any kind for any reason. This, while it could be the best policy, seems to contradict what is allowed in the Old Testament concerning borrowing. When allowed, the lender was to charge no interest of his fellow-countrymen.

So what does Paul intend as his message in *Romans 13.8*? Anytime there is a question concerning the meaning or application of a verse, we must turn to the context and consider the surrounding evidence. While this verse can be applied to loans and personal indebtedness, that is not the primary concern.

The passage deals with relationships between believers and those in authority over them. *Verse 1* says, "Let every soul be subject unto the higher powers. For there is no power but of God: the powers that be are ordained of God." Paul goes on to speak of how these leaders are ordained for our good to guard and protect those who have been placed under them.

In that respect, Paul gives four areas in which we should not be deficient in our support of those in authority (*Romans 13.7*). The first area concerns *"tribute."* The tribute equates to property taxes or direct taxes on things and even people. The *"custom"* was a transport tax, similar to modern tariffs that concerned commerce. Some have made light of our need to be submissive to authority, but that is exactly what is intended by the word *"fear."* It specifically refers to a reverence toward superiors. The final of the four areas is that of *"honor."* This specifically applies to people of distinction. We must show them due respect.

Concerning tribute, although it may be less than pleasurable to write a large check at the beginning of a year to pay our taxes – we must. If the laws can be changed, all the better, but no one has the right to simply ignore the law.

When Jesus was approached about His taxes, He chose an unusual method of obtaining the needed money. He had it delivered by a fish, but our Lord and Savior made no disparaging remarks nor did He make excuses – He paid the amount owed. He submitted, with a sweet spirit, to the authority of His day because He knew it had been ordained by God the Father.

In a day when questioning authority seems to be fashionable, even in Christian circles, we need to be reminded that every authority has been placed in that position by God and is therefore to be honored by our submission. This submission is what Paul had in mind when he used the word *"fear,"* for *"fear"* alludes to those who carry the means to enforce the laws (i.e. law enforcement, armed forces, etc.). For those who love their nation and follow the laws, this fear will be a humble respect rather than a terror.

The final area of paying dues concerns those to whom honor is due. This speaks of those who hold positions of authority. Our response to those in leadership from the President down to our immediate superiors on the job, to pastors and elders, and even parents is to show them the respect they deserve because of their God-given position (*I Timothy 2.2*). It is one thing to submit out of duty, but something entirely different to do so with a sweet spirit.

Paul further nails this by saying that the only thing we should owe anyone is Christian love. If attitudes are such that they take us to a point where we do not pay our dues to others, then our love life will be greatly affected. Pray for God's forgiveness and ask Him to grant to you a sweetly submissive spirit so that, in your life, you can exalt the precious name of our Savior. After all, if the world can tell we are Christians by our love, certainly they can tell our love by our attitudes and actions.

The Curse, Job 1.21

"And said, Naked came I out of my mother's womb, and naked shall I return thither: the LORD gave, and the LORD hath taken away; blessed be the name of the LORD." (Job 1.21)

In the Old Testament, the blessing was sought after by many individuals – including some who otherwise would seem to be uninterested in anything pertaining to the spiritual or religious. After Jacob had deceived and stolen Esau's birthright, Esau's plaintiff cry can almost be heard today. "But Father – what about me? Bless me, too!" (*Genesis 27.38*)

It was important enough that when Joseph brought his two sons, Ephraim and Manasseh, to Jacob for his blessing, Joseph tried to switch Jacob's hands so that the right hand would be on the elder and the left on the younger. Jacob, however, would have none of this switching. He intentionally wanted the greater blessing to fall on the younger grandson (*Genesis 48.15-20*).

Even heathen kings understood something of this blessing. Barak went to great lengths to hire Balaam as his prophet of doom in order to have an "edge" in battle against Israel. Barak believed a curse would bring Israel down, but God only allowed blessing (*Numbers 22.6, 12*).

The word translated **bless** in the Old Testament, interestingly enough, is the Hebrew word **barak**. It is used 289 times and is, with very few exceptions, translated *"bless"* (or *"blessed, blesseth, etc."*). **Barak** is also translated as *"kneel down" (Genesis 24.7)*, *"salute" (I Samuel 13.10; 25.14; II Kings 4.29; 10.15; 25.14)*, *"thanked" (II Samuel 14.22)*, *"congratulate" (II Chronicles 18.10)*, *"kneeled down" (II Chronicles 6.13)*, *"shall be praised" (Psalm 72.15)*, and *"kneel" (Psalm 95.6)*. There are two ways **barak** is translated that seem to be euphemistically applied. In each case, context delineates how the word is to be understood.

For example, in *I Kings 21.10 and 13*, **barak** is rendered *"blaspheme"* by the King James Translators because of the surrounding context. There, Jezebel is seeking to find someone to falsely accuse Naboth of blasphemy. Since Naboth was an upright man, she had the accusers use his words of blessing against him by suggesting that the words Naboth used were sarcastic or flippant; therefore, they took lightly the authority of God and the King. Paul warns that we should not let our good be evil spoken of (*Romans 14.16*). Naboth's own godly vocabulary was used against him.

Another instance of the use of **barak** that seems out of the ordinary is in *Job 1* and *2*. On four occasions the word **barak** is translated *"curse."* All but one has contextual support for that specific translation. In *Job 1.5*, we see Job offering sacrifices for his children, sanctifying them, lest they *"have sinned, and cursed (**barak**) God in their hearts."* This is similar to what Jezebel accused Naboth of when she claimed irreverence and flippancy on his part.

Twice, Satan confronted God with the assertion that if God *"touched"* Job, Job would in turn curse (**barak**) God (*Job 1.11; 2.5*). Satan must have believed that, since God had *"put a hedge"* around Job, he had become soft and spoiled. He further asserted that if God took these things from him, he would become flippant and irreverent toward God; but, *"in all this, Job sinned not, nor charged God foolishly." (Job 1.22)*

A bit of difficulty arises from *Job 2.9* concerning Job's wife and her statement. She uses the word **barak** which most often is translated *"curse"* in this verse which implies that she is so affected by her husband's affliction that she just wants to put an end to it. It has also been suggested that she was neither sympathetic toward him nor his condition and that she did what Satan supposed Job would do.

Lest we forget, there is no mention of Job's having a new wife at the end of the story when he is blessed with ten more children. This would suggest that she was still on the scene and experiencing the blessing of children and prosperity – although a quiet bystander. We must remember too, that Job was in such a terrible state of affliction that his friends did not recognize him (*Job 2.12*) and it took them a week of being in his presence for them to gather enough courage to speak with him at all (*Job 2.13*). Many have frustrated reactions when they do not understand the affliction of the righteous or the hand of God as He tests His children.

Yes, at least Job's wife stuck with him to the end. I will not speculate, but it is interesting that those who so harshly accuse Job's wife of being a curse left to him when he had lost all, do not recognize her quiet submission to his rebuke. After his rebuke at her flippancy and irreverence, she accepted her husband's word and went about her task around the home.

It could easily fit into the narrative for her to tell Job, "It's not worth it. Make peace with God and commit yourself into His hands." Although this is a minority opinion and a very uncommon view of a common verse, it fits nicely into the facts of the story; and, it fits the general usage of the word.

Job's rebuke was not that she wanted to curse God, but that she was willing to give up in the face of hardships and trials (*Job 1.21*). Many Christians find themselves in the same situation – when things go well they praise God, but when things go badly they accuse God of not being fair. It behooves each who claims Christ as Lord to give Him the benefit of the doubt and praise Him in good times and in bad.

Was the Second Day Good? Genesis 1.6-8

"And God said, Let there be a firmament in the midst of the waters, and let it divide the waters from the waters. And God made the firmament, and divided the waters which *were* under the firmament from the waters which *were* above the firmament: and it was so. And God called the firmament Heaven. And the evening and the morning were the second day." (Genesis 1.6-8)

The book of Genesis has been considered by most Bible students to be the Book of Beginnings. In those beginnings, a student will find foundational truths and principles that will aid in his understanding of the rest of God's Word. As I study the Bible and Genesis in particular, quite often thoughts seem to jump at me – sometimes because of what is said, but sometimes because of what is not said.

The last of those is what caught my attention in *Genesis 1.6-8*. In *Genesis 1* God gives His accounting of the days of creation from His perspective. What is peculiar to the second day is the silence of the Almighty by not pronouncing this day to be good. The Hebrew word for **good** is **tob**. Specifically it refers to something that is seen to fit into God's perfect plan and to glorify Him as God.

While no one can be dogmatic on the points that follow, they seem to make sense in the overall scheme of things. When I commented to some friends concerning God's silence on this particular occasion, the response was one that I had heard for some time. That when God was finished, He said *"...it was very good..." (Genesis 1.31)*. Quite honestly, that may be the answer, but it just did not satisfy my understanding.

From comparing Scripture with Scripture, I came to a conclusion that fits the various scenarios that needed to be satisfied. On the first day of creation, God spoke light into existence. Light, of course in our understanding, means the absence of darkness which in turn makes one able to see. It also refers to the light from the pillar of fire that led the Israelites (*Exodus 13.21*) and to the light from someone's face (meaning someone's favor, *Psalm 44.3*).

29

It can also be quickly understood that the angels are creatures that represent light and that they were created specifically to minister to man and were created prior to man. They are creatures of light. The thought of angels being created on the first day of creation fits nicely into the formula of creation. So when God said, *"Let there be light,"* He created all forms of light – including creatures of light – the angels.

Scripture also teaches that some of the angels chose to go against God and leave their first estate *(responsibilities, Jude 1.6)*. Since it was the angels' responsibility to be **good** (**tob** – *"to fulfill God's purpose"*) and to minister to God's creation (especially the saved, *Hebrews 1.14*), by leaving their position, God then relegated the evil ones to the domain of the skies. The Bible says that Satan is the prince and power of the air *(Ephesians 2.2)*.

If, in fact, Satan rebelled quickly after his creation, and God judged him quickly by removing his domain from that of the surface of the earth and removed him to the air; this judgment could have occurred on the second day. Later, this would be significant in the temptation of the first couple as Satan attempts to regain lost territory *(Ezekiel 28.13, 14)*.

The reason the second day was not said to be good was that it was the occasion of the first sin and God's first judgment on sin. Satan was removed from being God's anointed cherub and relegated to the firmament which God had separated from the earth. Satan had been the anointed cherub that *"covereth." (Ezekiel 28.14)* The word **covereth** is the same word used of the cherubim whose wings covered the Ark of the Covenant in the Holy of Holies. Satan was originally created to cover, or protect, the earth and to see to its proper administration.

Another question that must be addressed is in the light of this information. How could God pronounce all of creation very good if sin and judgment had occurred? Remembering that God is not the creator of sin, and it was not a good thing for Satan to sin; it remains true that man needed to have his free will tested. Since Satan had chosen a path of rebellion, and God knew he would test the first couple, God could easily say that, all things considered, this was very good. As is seen many times in Scripture, because of God's wisdom and foreknowledge, and because of Satan's limited knowledge, Satan played into God's hand (*I Corinthians 2.8*).

Since Adam and Eve chose to disobey God, they gave back to Satan territory that had been taken from him (*John 12.31; 14.30; 16.11*). It is comforting to know that God knew what Satan was doing all along and that His plan includes a full redemption for all His creation when He comes to the earth to set up His kingdom (*Revelation 12.10; II Peter 3.7-13*).

All of Satan's attempts and works will fade into obscurity when King Jesus takes command of His creation. From His throne in the New Jerusalem, the King will look into eternity past and future and say, *"This is very good!"*

Cherubim, Fire, and Sword, Genesis 3.24

"So he drove out the man; and he placed at the east of the garden of Eden Cherubims, and a flaming sword which turned every way, to keep the way of the tree of life." (Genesis 3.24)

Most often when we consider this verse, we suppose that God had placed those Cherubim at the eastern entrance to the Garden of Eden, wielding swords, and turning in every direction to bar the entrance so that the evicted couple would be unable to return and to take of the Tree of Life. It is a fact that the Cherubim were so placed, but the Bible is clear that the sword is quite independent of the guardians. As a matter of consideration, we should take a careful look at each of these three parts and learn some special spiritual lessons from them.

The cherubim were specialized angels that God created for the purpose of oversight and protection. Speaking specifically of the King of Tyre and symbolically of Satan, the prophet refers to them as *"...the anointed cherub that covereth." (Ezekiel 28.14)*. The word **covereth** indicates the role of a protector as the wings of the cherubim covered the Ark of God (*Exodus 25.22; Numbers 7.89*).

Ezekiel indicates that special power and privilege had been given to Satan (who, it seems, controlled the King of Tyre); but both privilege and power were taken away when he rebelled against God's plan and authority.

It is this type of angel that God placed at the entrance to the Garden of Eden. The cherubim who still fulfill God's intended plan are vital throughout Scripture. They can be seen associated with Ezekiel's vision (*Ezekiel 10*); with God's movements from place to place; (*II Samuel 22.11; Psalm 18.11*); and with God's presence to which man can approach (*Ezekiel 25.22; Numbers 7.89*). While similar to seraphim, they are, in fact, unique in that they show a power for protection while the seraphim show adoration due God's person (*Isaiah 6.2, 3*).

When considered with other available Scripture, the cherubim were at the Garden's entrance and, as a general rule, placed to point toward the majesty of the One on high. They would not allow approach in an irreverent fashion. While the seraphim used hot coals to purify Isaiah's lips (*Isaiah 6.6, 7*), it is the cherubim who dispenses them at God's command (*Ezekiel 10.27*).

In *Genesis 3*, the flame and the sword seem to be inseparable and a part of each other. Both are independent of the cherubim but connected to each other. The term used for *"flaming"* is unique to this verse but carries the idea of something that gleams or flashes. Other related words are used to indicate God's glory – that glory we refer to as the Shekinah glory of God. It was expressed to Moses at the burning bush (*Exodus 3.2*); on Mt. Sinai when God gave the Law (*Exodus 19.18*); and in the camp of the Israelites (specifically between the cherubim in the Holy of Holies and over the Tabernacle). It was that presence of God, which led the Israelites to the Promised Land and dwelled among them.

While most who read *Genesis 3.24* suppose the sword was a weapon used by the cherubim to keep all from going into the Garden by order of death, we may find an uncommon application. Paul reminds us that the Sword of the Spirit is the Word of God (*Ephesians 6.17*), and John records the fact that the Word of God is Jesus Christ Himself (*Job 1.1-5*).

Could it be possible that the cherubim were stationed outside the Garden to protect man from going out of the Way and at the same time pointing them to the true Way. It seems that when Adam and Eve were evicted, they would need somewhere to meet God, to offer sacrifices, and to worship.

In that place, just outside the Garden, God in His personal manifestation through the pre-incarnate Christ, revealed Himself to fallen man. He did not leave Adam and Eve alone nor did He allow them to wander hopelessly or aimlessly with no direction. There, at the entrance, Jesus Christ (pre-incarnated Christophany), as the Sword of the Spirit spoke face-to-face with Adam and Eve and received sacrifice from the repentant pair.

The cherubim, flame, and Sword were not placed as punitive, but were so placed for direction and accessibility to God through the only Way of approach. It seems that we forget that the only Way to approach God is through Christ Jesus (*John 14.6*).

Before, while in innocence, they walked together in the cool of the evening; but now, they approached His throne of grace seeking help in time of need. The pattern was laid that day that shows God's gracious offering of fellowship to any who will approach Him in the appropriate fashion. Today, we draw near to His throne as little children seeking this kind of treatment of our heavenly Father – knowing that we can do so because of the Way made clear by our Lord Jesus Christ.

Green Pastures, Psalm 23.2

"He maketh me to lie down in green pastures: he leadeth me beside the still waters. (Psalm 23.2)

Today I attended a memorial service for a man who was obviously quite godly. He had left a legacy of truth and righteousness that was superseded only by his love and compassion for others. As I settled back to listen to his pastor give his remarks, I was almost lulled to relaxation when he began reading from an old favorite – *Psalm 23*. After all, that is a common (albeit wonderful) passage from which to read when we want assurance that our Lord is with us and tenderly caring for His sheep.

One of his comments from *verse 2* especially pricked my attention when he mentioned the green pastures. At first he asked, "Why would sheep be lying down in green pastures?" Why, indeed?

Later I did a quick word study to determine what the author (King David) meant by green pastures. The word **green** is a word that refers to new growth or fresh sprouts. In observing my own sheep and horses, I have noticed that they will go for the new growth first. It must be that the new growth is the most tender and sweet.

The word **pasture** is taken from another Hebrew word that means *"home"* and refers to a place of quiet habitation and solicitude. Pastures figuratively refer to a pleasant place in which the sheep feel safe.

While it is quite understandable for sheep to lie down peacefully in a safe and calm environment; I have found that they tend to be eating machines on legs. Most of the time, they will stop eating only to chew their cud when they are completely satisfied.

Psalm 23 pictures for us how our precious Lord tends to His sheep. While in His care, nothing can harm us nor frighten us. He takes us into a place where, in Him, we are completely satisfied. It is only those who stray from His tender love that find themselves in peril on the crags and in distress.

As believers in Christ, we often are satisfied in knowing that our sins are forgiven and that we are on our way to heaven. Our Shepherd offers so much more. In describing this, the Apostle Paul tells us that He "*...is able to do exceeding abundantly above all that we ask or think...*"

We look for water to soothe our thirst in the heat of the day – He gives an endless supply of cool water that is still and easily assessable. We look for sustenance – he offers a protected place of quietness in which we can be completely satisfied.

Did I mention that the word **still** means more than a lack of motion? It suggests a resting place of quietness. Jesus is truly our good Shepherd. He provides, protects, and even pampers those who trust in Him.

The Lion and the Lamb, Revelation 5.4, 5

"And I wept much, because no man was found worthy to open and to read the book, neither to look thereon. And one of the elders saith unto me, Weep not: behold, the Lion of the tribe of Juda, the Root of David, hath prevailed to open the book, and to loose the seven seals thereof." (Revelation 5.4, 5)

Many people believe that *Revelation 4.1* (this author included) refers to the Rapture of the Church. When John saw the door opened in heaven, he was called to come and he immediately found himself in God's throne room. The picture is very similar to the one Isaiah witnessed in his record (*Isaiah 6*).

All around were things that dazzled John's mind – far more than he ever could have imagined. He saw the throne of the Almighty with the attending seraphim (described as beasts). He saw beautiful jewels, the sea of glass, and elders dressed in white. All present were there in tribute and honor of the King of kings. Additionally, the display was enhanced by a grand coruscation that was reminiscent of the lightning and thunder that had surrounded Mt. Sinai when God met with Moses.

When John finally regained some of his composure, he saw a scroll which was most probably the title deed to the universe. It had been sealed with seven seals representing the work of the Holy Spirit in His protective work over the earth. Although it was time for the book to be opened and God's judgment to be unleashed upon the world, there was no one found worthy in the great conclave of elders and angels who could open the book. John wept at the prospect of God's divine will being hindered.

At that moment, one of the elders called out to John and said, *"Weep not; behold, the Lion of the tribe of Judah, the root of David, hath prevailed to open the book and to loose the seven seals thereof." (Revelation 5.5)* As John looked up, past the elders, past the beasts, he saw, in the midst of the throne a Lamb standing. He alone was shown to be worthy to take away the seals and open the book.

Many things are poignant in these two verses. First, the elder invited John to look at the Lion – John saw the Lamb. Scripture reveals the Lord Jesus Christ in both capacities. To the world of unbelievers, in the end of the ages, He will be seen as a conquering, devastating, ferocious lion. When it is time, He will march forth into the world conquering all who oppose Him. To the believers, He is, was, and always shall be the Lamb of God that takes away the sins of those who trust in Him.

This is a matter of viewpoint. While the world looks at the Savior as a good man or a martyr who died for a cause, one day they will see Him in all of His glory as He splits the eastern sky with a vengeance. At the same time all who trust in Him will see Him as the One Who shed His blood for their redemption (*I Peter 2.7*).

There is something more in the picture of the Lion/Lamb. The Lion is depicted as a mature lion that is capable of destruction, but the Lamb referred to is diminutive meaning a small, baby lamb. Further, the phrase *"...it had been slain..."* refers to a violent and savage slaughter of innocent blood (*I John 3.12*). The Septuagint uses this term in reference to animal sacrifices (*Exodus 12.6*).

Specifically, the Lamb bears the visage of One slain for our sins. He was slaughtered by the hands of wicked men and the wounds still bear the appearance of freshness. So then, before the throne of the Almighty, the blood is still potent, and sufficient, vital, and powerful. It is today exactly what it was when it was first shed. As the hymn writer says, *"It shall never lose its power."*

A commentator for the Peoples New Testament says, "John looked to see this mighty one who was deemed worthy to exercise the prerogative of God. But he appears . . . as a Lamb of God slain for sins; a sacrificial Lamb bearing wounds, the marks of having been slain. The Lion had become a Lamb. The Lamb became a Lion, a conqueror, and 'prevailed' so as to be able to hold and open the book, or to hold the reins of all power by submitting unto death." (*The People's New Testament*. B. W. Johnson, 1891.)

"There is a fountain filled with blood drawn from Emmanuel's veins;

And sinners plunged beneath that flood lose all their guilty stains.

Dear dying Lamb, Thy precious blood shall never lose its power
Till all the ransomed church of God be saved, to sin no more.

"E're since, by faith, I saw the stream Thy flowing wounds supply,
Redeeming love has been my theme, and shall be till I die.

"Lord, I believe Thou has prepared, unworthy though I be,
For me a blood bought free reward, a golden harp for me!

"'Tis strung and tuned for endless years, and formed by power divine,
To sound in God the Father's ears no other name but Thine."

Coals of Fire, Romans 12.20; Proverbs 25.21, 22

"Therefore if thine enemy hunger, feed him; if he thirst, give him drink: for in so doing thou shalt heap coals of fire on his head." (Romans 12.20)

I came across a verse, a common verse, the other day that again arrested my attention. Is it not wonderful how God's Word is forever fresh as we read it and meditate upon it?

Whether you pastor a church or are a member of a church, we often find great comfort in the thought that if I do right; God will take care of my enemies. Even the sweet psalmist of Israel (King David), after confessing God's goodness and greatness and confessing his own imperfections said, *"Do not I hate them, O LORD, that hate thee? And am not I grieved with those that rise up against thee? I hate them with perfect hatred: I count them mine enemies." (Psalm 139.21, 22)*

In *Psalm 58* David cried out to the Lord for deliverance from the wicked by asking God to break out their teeth (*Psalm 58.6*).

All of this seems to go contrary to the New Testament teaching given to us both by Jesus Himself and the Apostles. In *Matthew 5* our Lord said, *"Ye have heard that it hath been said, Thou shalt love thy neighbor, and hate thine enemy. But I say unto you, Love your enemies, bless them that curse you, do good to them that hate you, and pray for them which despitefully use you and persecute you." (Matthew 5.43, 44)*

It seems that there had been some confusion among the general population concerning the proper application of Scripture. The thought was that they were responsible to love others only to a point. When others became enemies, they were no longer required to love them. This is common in our day – in our own Christian lives. We tend to pick and choose verses that help justify our actions and thereby give to us a false sense of righteousness.

But what about David's requirement of teeth and his assertion of hatred? The greatest problem with actually applying these concepts lies in a definition – or more pointedly in a distinction. Who are the ones that should be hated? If you return to both passages in Psalms, you will find that the ones to whom David referred were not considered to be his personal enemies – but God's enemies.

Even when fleeing for his life from Saul, when he had opportunity to take action and had the anointing from God on his life; David did not take matters into his own hands. He gave place for wrath (*Romans 12.19*).

David had the ability to distinguish between his personal enemies and God's enemies. Saul had become God's enemy and God had specifically taken His blessing from Saul and had ripped away Saul's kingdom.

David knew he had been anointed to be king of God's people; therefore, a threat to him was a threat to God. When Absalom was working his mischief in dividing the people's loyalties, David could honestly have compassion on his son and love him tenderly because he knew that God was in control. Absalom could not win.

And lest we forget, after Saul was off the scene, David called for any who were of the household of Saul to be brought to him. Mephibosheth, Jonathan's son, was the one found and brought to David. David brought him to the royal palace, fed him at the family table, and gave to him a glorious heritage with land and possessions (*II Samuel 9.5-9*). Although Mephibosheth was Saul's grandson, he had done nothing to derail God's plan. He was not God's enemy. Even though David had every right from a human standpoint to wipe out all that remained of Saul's house, he left that in God's hands.

It is a legitimate prayer to ask God to judge His enemies and to protect His children from hurt and persecution. It is also legitimate to ask for God to avenge Himself and His holy name from defilement by removing any who would do damage to His Person. But, here is the rub. We find it most difficult to distinguish between those who work iniquity and those who make personal attacks against us. The Bible is very clear that we are to bless those who curse us and do good to those who despitefully use us. The Apostle Paul adds more when he writes, *"See that none render evil for evil unto any man; but ever follow that which is good, both among yourselves, and to all men." (I Thessalonians 5.15)*

I am sure that by now you are asking, "What does all this have to do with 'coals of fire?'" Back to *Romans 12.20*. Within the context,

Paul is dealing with the perfect, human, living sacrifice. He tells us how to live and think in order to be pleasing to God and to fit into the community of Christians called the body of Christ. He exhorts each of us to live peaceably (the Greek suggests *"to make peace"*) with all men if at all possible. If it is not possible, the matter should be left completely to the Lord.

Many years ago a church member came to me to ask for my counsel concerning a particularly annoying neighbor. When I suggested he pray for the neighbor's salvation, the response was something like this: "I'm not sure I want him saved. I don't like him and I'd rather see God judge him." Not long after that, my friend was under deep conviction of his poor attitude and soon saw his neighbor become a brother in Christ.

But what happens when peace does not come? Does *Romans 12.20* give the answer? Yes, it does. As a matter of fact, it goes the extra mile. While, humanly speaking, I may find it easy to feed and clothe my enemy, send him on his way, and wait for God's vengeance; the implication of the coals of fire is quite different from our western interpretation.

In the Middle East, it is common, even today, for heavy burdens to be carried on one's head. It would not be at all uncommon for someone whose fire had gone out to seek live embers from a neighbor for the purpose of rekindling their flame. By heaping coals of fire on their head, essentially, they would be offering a double blessing. Even someone who is calloused would often offer something to the hungry, but to offer more than what is needed is to go far beyond the necessary to the point of inexplicable blessing.

When at times I would rather think like my friend and soothe my conscience by giving essentials to my enemies, here we are exhorted to go an extra step and offer a blessing. It is required that we give food and water. It is Christ-like to give unasked-for help that will bless. It is also Christ-like to see the enemy warmed and filled (*James 2.16*), and to see them go on their way having received a blessing from a truly loving Christian.

To watch that person go away while all the time waiting for God's judgment to fall would be against the character of our precious Savior Who came to seek and to save that individual. If we do anything else, we have fallen into a trap that will grow bitterness in our own lives. Some are trapped now – waiting, like Jonah, for the wrath of God to fall while God's Holy Spirit tries to encourage us to *". . .not be overcome of evil, but to overcome evil with good."*

Give a Blessing to the Enemies? Matthew 5.44

"But I say unto you, Love your enemies, bless them that curse you, do good to them that hate you, and pray for them which despitefully use you, and persecute you." (Matthew 5.44)

The word bless is a word that is thrown around rather flippantly these days. We ask someone to say a blessing over a meal or when someone sneezes, we say, "Bless you." (This in fact is a shorter version of "May God bless you.") During one graduation in a Kentucky school where the opponents of God forbade the use of the name God during the commencement ceremonies, students took it upon themselves to remedy the situation. At an appointed time several of the graduating seniors sneezed – to which hundreds in the audience responded with "God bless you!" May God truly bless all that were involved.

Although there are connections between these thoughts of blessing and *Matthew 5.44*, our Lord expects more than an "off the cuff" remark about someone's health. The blessing should never resemble a simple, common expression that is said out of habit. It is something that should be thought through and said intentionally.

In *Matthew 5.44*, the word translated **bless** is from the Greek word **eulogeo**. The prefix **eu** means *"good"* or *"well,"* and the main word is **logos** meaning *"word."* Put together it means *"to speak well of"* or *"to say a good word of"* – to bless.

As a child, I was often admonished by my parents with, "If you can't say something good about someone, it's better to say nothing at all." That is good advice but still stops short of what our Lord had in mind. He tells us to take an active role in blessing those that curse us. Those who curse you are those who wish something bad or evil to come your way that would destroy you.

It is easy enough to bless your friends and the ones who have just given you a birthday present, but to bless those who wish you harm is difficult indeed. But this has very little to do with us. In fact, it has everything to do with our testimony and our relationship with our

Lord. He goes on to insist that we actively seek to do the opposite of what our enemies are trying to do to us. To do well and pray with a sincere attitude of good will is what fulfills love's demands (*Matthew 5.46-48*).

In Biblical blessings, there seems to be at least three parts to a blessing. (For a clearer understanding, study the blessing of Isaac to Jacob and Jacob to his twelve sons – *Genesis 48 and 49.*) The first part of the blessing contains a commitment of the one giving the blessing.

I had the privilege of home-schooling my daughter for the last six years of her secondary education. At her graduation, I followed this guideline and told her that I was committed to her with my love and support. I encouraged her to follow the Lord's leading and even though I would hope and pray that she did right, my love for her would never be something she would need to question. After all, is that not the attitude our precious Savior adopted when He promised to bless believers with all spiritual blessing?

The second part of the blessing involves qualities and characteristics of the one receiving the blessing. Look again at Jacob's blessing of his children. He did not quickly pass a hand over the bunch and say, "God bless you." He named each one and pointed out their strengths and weaknesses. It is interesting how well he knew each of them. Not one said, "Hold on Dad, you have this all wrong!"

In order for a father or mother to invoke this part of the blessing, he must spend time with his children so that he knows them and they know him intimately. The first part of the blessing – the commitment – will be meaningless unless the child knows the parent is committed in more than word. The qualities and characteristics you chose must be ones that are really appropriate for the child.

The third part of the blessing is the best part. Here, the one offering the blessing asks God to bless the receiver. A good place to find some common elements to include in this prayer can be found in the prayer of Jabez (*I Chronicles 4.10*). I asked God to bless my daughter and to expand her coasts (her opportunities of service for Christ). After all, she will be going to college and I want her college education to enhance what she has learned about being a soul-winner and about being like Christ. I then asked God to keep her from evil – evil that she may do herself and evil that may come to her from the outside. Finally, I asked for God to go with her and that her steps would be ordered by her Lord.

So how does this all relate to my enemies? It would seem that the Scriptures require that we offer this same blessing to those who treat us badly. *"For if ye love them which love you, what reward have ye? Do not even the publicans (tax collectors) the same? And if ye salute (embrace, enfold, welcome) your brethren only, what do ye more than others? Do not the publicans so?"* (Matthew 5.46, 47)

Is the one who cuts in line at the supermarket an enemy? Is the one who turns in front of you on the highway an enemy? I must admit that my response is not always in the form of a blessing nor is my attitude.

God wants us to bless (say good things about) Him in every aspect of our lives – whether it is in actions, speech, or attitudes. He wants us to be perfect (*"complete, mature, and fully furnished"*) in our relationships. Maybe today would be a good time to begin blessing your enemies.

While reading this, no doubt someone has come to your mind. You could begin with small steps first. Find a nice card and write a special note following the three guidelines of a blessing. It does not matter whether this is a family member, co-worker, or neighbor. Write it today – now. Mail it and watch God begin to work.

Death and Judgment, Hebrews 9.27, 28

"And as it is appointed unto men once to die, but after this the judgment: So Christ was once offered to bear the sins of many; and unto them that look for him shall he appear the second time without sin unto salvation." (Hebrews 9.27 28)

It would seem that Enoch and Elijah have thrown a wrench into the interpretation of these verses for many students of God's Word. If *Hebrews 9.27* is to be understood as a strictly held rule, where do we put these two men? As a point of interest, where do we put the great multitude that will be caught up to be with Christ prior to His return?

Just as context is vital to understanding Scripture, so also is the syntax of each sentence. To make much of the fact that all die places the major emphasis of the sentence on the wrong clause. The most important part of the sentence involves *Hebrews 9.28*.

The argument of whether Enoch and Elijah must sometime die in the future in order to fulfill this verse is to miss the point of this illustration. Neither does the dogmatism that many hold (suggesting that the Rapture of the Church is some sort of death) fit this scenario.

By using *Hebrews 9.27* as a supportive word picture of *Hebrews 9.28*, many problems are overcome and a beautiful picture of our Lord's Word is revealed. The general condition in which man finds himself forces upon him the responsibility of facing separation from the mortal body in what is called death. It also causes us to face our future in terms of judgment.

More to the point, however, is the supreme sacrifice of the Lord Jesus Christ. As man dies once and is judged, so Christ died once and was judged. Each died a physical death and faced spiritual judgment.

In the case of man, he must pay for his sin. That payment is exacted either from him personally by eternity in hell or from his account to which the Savior of the world offers sufficient payment through His blood sacrifice to satisfy every sin. Man, after all, is sinful.

As man only dies once, so Christ died only once. Christ died to provide payment for man's sin, but it remains that He died once. This is the subject of these verses. Not that every man must die, but that payment has been made.

The last part of *Hebrews 9.28* gives the promise of a wonderful blessing to those who *"look for"* (*"eagerly and expectantly await"*) His appearing. While on the cross, He bore our sins in His own body and paid the price for all who would believe; when He returns, He will do so without (*"in a place separate from"*) sin unto salvation.

We should never become so preoccupied with the fact that death is all around that we lose sight of the awesome prospect of life through Christ. The judgment that once would frighten humanity because it would be faced apart from help has been taken away because Christ died once for all and He will return apart from sin to gather His saved to Himself. The saved will ever be with the Lord – without (*"in a different place from"*) their sin. Those sins will never be brought back again but are completely gone.

Thank God for His wonderful gift of salvation.

The Bride Wore White, Revelation 19.8

"And to her was granted that she should be arrayed in fine linen, clean and white: for the fine linen is the righteousness of saints." (Revelation 19.8)

A part of the present work of Christ through the Holy Spirit in the world today is to prepare His bride so that she is a glorious church *"not having spot nor wrinkle" (Ephesians 5.22)*. In the end, the bride will be dressed in righteousness – the righteousness of the saints. In order to see this prospect, we must go back and visit the illustrations God gives as examples.

What the Bible teaches in the Old Testament is given for examples that help us learn and put together God's plan. Even in the Levitical priesthood, God showed the separation that exists between those upon whom God's blessing rests and those upon whom it does not.

The priests had two coverings. On the inside, next to the priest's body, those in the priesthood wore a common, flaxen cloth. This cloth was to cover their nakedness (*Exodus 28.42*). It needed not to be fancy, but utile. While it was used to describe the ephod worn by Samuel and some other priests (*I Samuel 2.18; 22.18*), it was not what was seen as an outside garment while the priests were serving the Lord.

On the outside of the clothing was a robe of white. It too was linen, but evidently had been bleached so as to reflect the brilliance of the sun. This may have been, in some way, an attempt by the priests to emulate the coruscation evidenced upon Moses after he had spent time in the personal presence of God while receiving the commandments on Mount Sinai. As they stood before the laver and altar, they would have reflected a brightness that would also symbolize their piety.

The Old Testament priest is an example (type) of the New Testament believer (*Revelation 1.6; 5.10; 20.6*). Since the New Testament believer has the privilege to go directly to God in prayer through Jesus Christ (*I Timothy 2.5*), all true believers are priests and stand before God in garments of white. Although we are clothed in worldly garments (pictured by the plain flaxen garments of the priests), we stand before God in brilliant white that has been bleached by the blood of the Lamb of God.

Essentially, when God looks at His children, He sees only the reflection of the Son because our dinginess is replaced by His glory. Our vileness is replaced by His perfection. Our drabness is replaced by His brilliance. Today, the believer stands personally before God in worship and for prayer because of the new robe of righteousness provided as our covering by Christ so that we can stand as perfect in the presence of the Almighty God.

But, there is more. With both the Old Testament Levitical priest and the New Testament believer-priest, the brilliance is a reflection of the glory of God. God has promised to enact a New Covenant with the reunited house of Israel. That New Covenant will take the outside brightness and place it within the heart of God's people so that they will shine from within (*Jeremiah 31.31-34*).

After the Rapture of the Church (New Testament believers – *Revelation 4.1*), and after the Marriage Supper of the Lamb and the Great Tribulation (*Revelation 19.1*) the Bride of Christ will have become His wife (*Revelation 19.7*). At that time the bride will be given new clothes – spotless white (*Revelation 19.8*).

John records that the Bride *"should be arrayed in fine linen, clean and white . . ." (Revelation 19.8).* Arrayed means to be clothed about or covered. Fine linen refers to the same type of garment that the priests wore, but this will become the clothing that is next to the person. All of the flaxen, plain cloth will be gone. The new garments will be clean – pure and without blemish or spot, as was promised by our Lord (*Ephesians 5.27*).

Throughout the Book of the Revelation the word translated **white** is the Greek word **leukos**. It is the same thought used of the Old Testament priests – *"white, shining, and glittering."* Only in *Revelation 15.6* and *19.8* does the writer use a different word – **lampros**. **Lampros** is the word from which we get the word *lamp*. It indicates brilliance from a source that is within the lamp.

Powered from within by the Spirit of God, the Bride of Christ will glow with the presence of the Almighty. Now the believer can, through devotion and godly living, show to the world the power of

God by reflecting His majesty. We are still in a dingy mantel that shadows the perfect Light. When we are, one day, clothed in His righteousness, stripped of this vile flesh, the glory of His presence will shine forth from a pure heart and body for all to see clearly.

Sons of God, Genesis 6.4

"There were giants in the earth in those days; and also after that, when the sons of God came in unto the daughters of men, and they bare *children* to them, the same *became* mighty men which *were* of old, men of renown." (Genesis 6.4)

Much has been written concerning the *"sons of God"* in this Genesis passage and although the term for **sons** (**ben**) in the Hebrew occurs over 5,000 times, because of its connection with the term *"of God"* (***elohim***) in three specific settings in Scripture, it has drawn much attention. Two of the settings are in the book of Job (*Job 1.6; 2.1; 38.7* – the first two verses are the same basic setting).

The various interpretations of *Genesis 6.4* fall into three major lines of thought. The most obscure of all is an attempt at making the sons of God to be people of royal descent and the daughters of men commoners. From this interpretation, some have proposed that the cause for the giants was the intermarrying between royalty and subjects. This suggestion has fallen largely by the wayside because it is nearly impossible to make it fit into practical exegetical interpretation. In other words, this line of thinking just does not make sense.

A second line of thought proposes that these sons of God were actually fallen angels who took control of human bodies or else somehow became humans in order to procreate with human beings. We must admit that many good men have taken this position with much of their foundational material based on *Job 38.7* and the fact that giants are mentioned in the same context as the sons of God and daughters of men in *Genesis 6.4.*

There are several problems with this position. The first is from an assumption made in *Matthew 22.30, "For in the resurrection they neither marry, nor are given in marriage, but are as the angels of God in heaven."* This suggests that the angels in heaven do not procreate. How then could they produce a race of giants?

Those holding this position suggest that they either possessed human bodies or that they made themselves to appear as humans. In the first case, the offspring would still be human, and in the second case, there could be no co-habitation.

Another thought that must be considered is the fact that whatever this problem was, it had affected the entire human race (*Genesis 6.5*). This was a global problem of pandemic proportions. Since Noah and his family were the only ones to be spared (including all air-breathing animals), the demons must have co-habitated with every man, woman, child, and animal. This seems to be completely beyond the realm of possibility.

So then, we are left with only one other possibility. This supposition gives the idea that the sons of God must be recognized in its common sense as followers of and believers in the One true God while the daughters of men must be the offspring of unbelievers. In order to hold to this interpretation, several questions must be answered and support must be given.

The major objection seems to be in the interpretation and application of the two settings in the book of Job. In *Job 1 and 2*, the scene does not seem to be one in heaven but on earth. The context is clearly indicative of a worship service that Job, as a community elder, is leading. This is not a unique suggestion because Job was very careful to offer appropriate sacrifices for his family (*Job 1.4, 5*) and was asked of God to offer sacrifices for his associates (*Job 32.4*).

The context, then, shows that Job was leading a community worship service where the local believers (*sons of God*) gathered to sacrifice to God. It is to this place that Satan turns his attention looking for something that will bring shame to the gathering.

It is not difficult to envision that where God's people gather, there the hosts of heaven and the unseen hosts of the world gather for inspection. Satan had answered God's questions by saying that he had been going around the world. What he did not readily admit was that he was seeking someone to devour (*I Peter 5.8*).

A more difficult passage to put into a human perspective is in *Job 38.7*. There, the immediate context of the verse suggests that the *"morning stars"* and the *"sons of God"* should go together. The surrounding verses would suggest something different.

God is reprimanding Job for not giving Him glory in creation and preservation. Job had tried to justify himself rather than God. God asked Job a series of questions that Job was unable to answer. Some of them dealt with creation but not all of them. The assumption that all questions deal with creation limits the scope of the interrogation.

After drawing Job's attention to a broad range of questions, God asked Job where he was when the *"morning stars" (angels)* sang and the *"sons of God" (believers)* shouted for joy. All the time Job was lamenting his position – he should have been exalting God rather than defending his own position. In the final exhortation of Elihu and the rebuffing by God, exalting God was the subject. The angels of God sang and true believers rejoiced in God's greatness.

With all that in mind, we must return to *Genesis 6* to complete this study. In the context, a careful study of *Genesis 4* will show the ungodly line of people who were descendents of Cain. Cain, because of his refusal to repent, was exiled to the land of Nod. Neither he nor his descendents were to mix with the rest of humanity.

Genesis 5 follows the godly line that, after their progenitor Shem, began to call upon the name of God. This line was to follow God, stay separate from Cain (the world), and raise a godly generation. They did not.

A special key is given to help us understand the specific meaning and application of this passage. The Bible says that the *sons of God* saw the *daughters of men* as being ***fair***. The word ***fair*** is translated from the Hebrew word **tob** which means *"something that is good and fulfills God's intended purpose."* It is the same word used to describe God's approval of creation. It was very **good** (**tob**). It is also used to contrast the difference between **good** (**tob**) and **evil** (**ra'ah** – *"that which is outside the good and perfect will of God*) and is the descriptive name for the Tree of the Knowledge of Good (**tob**) and Evil (**ra'ah**).

The great problem that had become the norm for the day was that God's people, rather than maintaining their godly separation, looked at the things of the world as having the potential for fulfilling God's purpose. In other words, they saw the world as being good. We should remember that each time in history, when man thought he could present whatever he wanted to God, rather than what God had specifically selected; judgment fell. It separated Cain to a place apart from fellowship. It caused destruction in Lot's life as he sat in the gates of the city of Sodom. It brought rejection to the Pharisees who offered their outward purity rather than God's holiness.

The same attitude permeates much of Christianity today; people who claim Christ as Savior are wanton in their devotion to God and separation from the world. Do not be deceived – God will accept nothing less than the best. None of our own offerings are good enough. Each person must come to God through the blood of Jesus Christ and must be accepted only on that basis. We must have no other claim and must offer no other argument for justification. We, as followers of Christ, must separate ourselves from the world and its attitudes and cling tenaciously to the righteousness of Christ Jesus. He is our only hope and plea.

700 Left-Handed Men, Judges 20.16

"Among all this people *there were* seven hundred chosen men lefthanded; every one could sling stones at an hair *breadth,* and not miss." (Judges 20.16)

Israel was on the brink of civil war because of a horrific sin that committed in Gibeah, four miles north of Jerusalem (for background information read *Judges 19*). The reaction to that sin and the arrogance on the part of the Benjamites had brought their army of 26,000 (plus 700 from Gibeah, *Judges 20.15*) against the formidable army of the rest of Israel (numbering 400,000).

At first glance it would certainly seem either a remarkable step of faith or an absurdly insane move on Benjamin's part to try to stand against such a foe. There must be a strong reason for taking such a stand.

All involved in this fray were considered men of war who could handle themselves well and who could use a sword – all except for 700 unusual men who used non-conventional weapons. These men were all left-handed and their weapon of choice was a sling.

The left-handed men have been described in many ways from ambidextrous war heroes to one-armed farmers. From the original Hebrew, we get a truly uncommon view of some common verses.

In the English, left-handed is one, hyphenated word, but in the Hebrew it is made up of three words. The Hebrew phrase is *"itter yadyemeeno"* which could be translated literally as *"impeded in the right hand."* ***Itter*** is an adjective indicating left-handedness. It is also used to describe Ehud, a judge in Israel. ***Yad*** is a feminine noun meaning *"hand or strength."* It appears often in the Old Testament in literal, figurative, and technical uses. Metaphorically, it signifies strength or power (*Deuteronomy 32.36; Isaiah 37.27*) and authority or right to possess (*Genesis 16.9; II Chronicles 13.16*). Finally, the word ***yemeeno*** generally refers to the right hand, or as here implies, the *"hand of power."*

Although some would suggest that these men were *"one-handed,"* that is not the implication from the Hebrew. Here we learn that these 700 men simply had their strength in their left hand. In many situations, being strong on the opposite side of the standard would give a great advantage. A boxer facing a *"south-paw"* (**yemeeno** may also mean *"to the south"*) must adjust his stance and style. A marksman with a firearm has a difficult time firing his weapon around the left side of a barricade. A left-handed shooter in basketball finds that the defender must adjust his tactics in order to be effective when defending his shot.

The left-handed men were extremely proficient at using a sling. Remember that David slew Goliath with a sling. The Bible says that the stone sank in the giant's head (*I Samuel 17.49*) which indicates that it was delivered with considerable force. It also suggests that it could be delivered with deadly accuracy. The verse says that they could *"sling a stone at a hair and not miss."* That may be where the phrase *"splitting hairs"* originated.

Adding to this prowess is the understanding that some of the best slingers of antiquity were from the islands of Majonca and Minorca. Part of the rights of passage for their children was when they were forced into a fast until they were able to strike bread from the top of a pole or from another distant object. Only upon completion of this requirement was the fast over because they had won their meal. It is reported that proficient slingers were accurate at distances as far as 600 feet.

A question remains. If these men were proficient in war (*II Chronicles 26.14*) and the other 26,700 were men of war, why would this group go against the vast army of Israel with 400,000 troops? When a person or a people become calloused toward their own sin and seek to justify themselves, they will go to extreme measures to cover their tracks. Benjamin and Gibeah were willing to kill and die in battle, against all known wisdom, in order to keep from confessing their coldness and hardness toward God and in regard to sin.

In the final tally, Benjamin went home with only 700 men (possibly the 700 left-handed men). They lost 26,000 in battle. Had they been open with God and with their peers, this catastrophe could have been avoided. Rather than confess, they fought and lost.

Every time someone tries to cover his sins, it costs dearly – it costs those who are close and it harms the cause of Christ. It may cost today – tomorrow – or later; but it will cost. God is looking for people with tender, contrite hearts who will quickly confess and forsake sin. In the short-run and in the long-run, it is the only way to peace and longevity.

Can Iron Swim? II Kings 6.6

"And the man of God said, Where fell it? And he shewed him the place. And he cut down a stick, and cast *it* in thither; and the iron did swim." (II Kings 6.6)

Several years ago I was helping my father-in-law on his farm. We were tearing down and rebuilding some fences that were in desperate need of repair. As a young man I had very few tools of my own so I borrowed some from my brother-in-law. Among them was a pair of lineman pliers that would cut through the thick fence wire. My father, who used a similar tool while working for the telephone company, simply called them "nines" because they were nine inches long.

We had worked most of the morning and as I began cutting through one of the strands, I heard a strange pop. The pop was not the sound of the pliers cutting through the wire but the sound of one side of the pliers snapping under the pressure.

Your experiences may not be like mine. You may have had wonderful experiences in borrowing and lending, but mine seem to normally bring me to a place of replacing the borrowed item. In reality, I would find myself buying two tools instead of one – one for me and one to replace the one I had damaged.

Quite often the reason for borrowing is a lack of sufficient funds with which to purchase the item. When I was in college and seminary I found that many wants were unavailable even though God was gracious in supplying all my needs.

II Kings 6 brings us to a scene at a seminary where the sons of the prophets were studying. The school was evidently a boarding school and the student body had outgrown the facility. The answer to the problem was the same that Booker T. Washington employed when building Tuskegee University – the students became the builders of additional facilities.

The training at the prophets' school taught the principles of God and also taught the students the value of good work ethics. As the young men were chopping down trees for timbers, one of the students lost his head – his axe head that is. It flew off the handle and landed in the river – out of sight and beyond reach.

He cried out in despair because it was borrowed and he obviously did not have the means to replace it. Before despair set in, the man of God threw a stick into the water and the *"iron did swim."*

Some would suggest that when the prophet determined the place where the axe head had fallen, he took a stick, thrust it into the water and subsequently the stick found the hole in the axe head. The man of God then simply lifted the head from the water. There is a problem with that interpretation because the word **cast** means *"to throw."* The stick left the man of God's hand. While some would deny the supernatural miracle that occurred there, true students of the Bible see God's provision by extra-natural methods.

The fact is that *"the iron did swim"* *(float)*. This is just a small cameo that shows God's provision for those who love Him. God's attention is always toward His children and He cares deeply for their welfare.

Being in the will of God, in sweet fellowship with Him, and walking in His footsteps will bring us into His divine protection. Nothing is lost of which He is not aware and that does not draw His interest. Never is there despair for which He does not enter into our lives with blessing. As His child, we can rest assured that God will provide. He may not cause your axe head to float, but He will be with you through every trial you face.

Emerods and Mice, I Samuel 6.5, 11

"Wherefore ye shall make images of your emerods, and images of your mice that mar the land; and ye shall give glory unto the God of Israel: peradventure he will lighten his hand from off you, and from off your gods, and from off your land." (I Samuel 6.5)

The Ark of God was in the wrong place with the wrong people – people who did not honor the Lord or the sacredness of life which is the blood. Jehovah Elohim, the only true God, was the God of the Israelites. He had delivered them from oppressors and had given them clear access to holiness by way of sacrifice. They could approach God Who dwelt between the Cherubim over the Mercy Seat which was the lid for the Ark.

This was a most holy place and the Israelite's sacred chest. It was to be in the Most Holy Place and to be viewed only once a year by the High Priest on the Day of Atonement. It was such a holy place that the High Priest was only allowed entrance after making sacrifice for his own sins. The Ark of the Covenant was so special that it was referred to as the "Ark of God's presence."

The Ark of God's presence had been removed from its holy place and taken to the battlefield as a "good luck charm." God will not be so used. He will be known as God the Almighty, but will not be denigrated to being considered a mere amulet against evil.

When the Philistines captured the Ark, they proceeded to add it to their collection of gods. They had no problem with this because, being polytheistic, one more god could only be a good thing. Almost immediately the Philistines put the Ark in the temple of one of their major gods – Dagon.

Dagon could not stand up to God. After all, Dagon was made of "stuff" – wood, metal, and stone. God created all the stuff from which Dagon was fashioned. In the morning, the Philistines found their god fallen on the ground and on his face.

They should have realized that if he were a real god he should have at least been able to right himself. He needed help. The Philistines set things back in order and left for the night. In the morning, Dagon was on the floor again but this time he was broken (*I Samuel 5.4*).

At this point things get interesting. Even after seeing the superiority of God over Dagon, the Philistines would not accept the fact that God is God and beside Him there is no other. Dagon could not deliver himself anymore than he could deliver the multitudes that worshipped him. One thing is still true today – man tends to cling to religion and traditions even though God and His power are everywhere evident.

After the Philistines made their reparations and thereby chose their god, God sent a plague of emerods and mice (possibly rats, too). The Hebrew word translated *emerods* in the Authorized Version has been variously translated as *"tumors, sores, and boils"* among other things. The intended meaning of the term suggests bleeding hemorrhoids. These sores would be more than simply uncomfortable – they would be debilitating.

Along with the hemorrhoids was a plague of mice (or rats) that carried diseases. Although the rat is not specifically mentioned in the Bible, they were as common in Canaan then as they are today. Archaeologists have uncovered rat bones in great numbers in all strata of the old Palestinian cities. Herodotus records an account of an invasion of mice into the army of Sennacherib which ultimately destroyed the army.

In attempts to appease Israel's "god," the Philistines made idols resembling what had conquered them – hemorrhoids and mice. One was made to correspond with each of the Philistine's lords (*I Samuel 6.17, 19*). They sent back to Israel, on a new cart drawn by milk cows, the Ark of God and the tokens of their distress – their concept of God.

As with so many people today, the Philistines missed the point. The Philistines were all concerned with being busy and working to keep their god in shape. God is concerned with a blood sacrifice. The bleeding hemorrhoids were given to remind them that man can only approach God through the blood. Even though the fighting men were brought to a complete stop, they did not repent or offer to God what He required of them. They sent God away.

The mice and rats brought disease and want, but the unbelievers still did not see the point. God was in their midst offering visual illustrations of their need and the means of being healed. They rejected.

Today, more and more, we see people of the world as they push away the true God of eternity who alone can heal and satisfy. Unbelievers in every area of life believe that if they can rid their world of God, all will be well. We are inundated with lawsuits and threats that promise problems if we preach or pray in public. Our Christian children are forced to take a stand in a very wicked world that would rather tell God to leave than have His peace in their lives. Their Dagon keeps falling on his face before the God of gods and the world keeps patching him up.

Several years ago at a public high school football game in South Carolina, I and my officiating crew stepped onto the field to begin our duties prior to the opening game of the season. New laws and opinions had been handed down to the various administrators requiring them to cease having prayer before athletic events. I had been to this school before and knew that the principal was a believer who personally led all present to God's throne of grace at each home game.

Even though he had been threatened with law suits and it was rumored that brass from the ACLU were present, the evening began as usual with one exception. The principal asked for all to rise as he prayed to the Almighty God of the universe invoking God's protection for the players and others who were involved (he even prayed for us – the game officials). Part of his opening statement went something like this: "I invite all of you to stand with me this evening as we seek God's face together in prayer. Tonight we have some special guests with us in the crowd from the ACLU. We would be delighted if you would join with us as we pray."

God give each of us courage to stand. Dear Heavenly Father, keep us from the error of sending You away while holding on to the gods of this world. Lord, help me to always be aware of the fact that salvation is only through the shed blood of Jesus Christ and give me the energy to never tire of telling others of Your wonderful salvation.

The Lamb, Exodus 12.1-5

"Your lamb shall be without blemish, a male of the first year: ye shall take *it* out from the sheep, or from the goats." (Exodus 12.5)

The Passover was declared to be a national holiday of feasting in commemoration of God's miraculous deliverance for Israel from Egyptian bondage. Since the first Passover was prepared in haste, eaten in haste, and the expulsion made in haste; Israel needed directions for later observance.

In these verses, the dates are first given that add a tremendous weight of importance to the observance. Israel's year was to be remembered by the deliverance from Egypt. Feasting and joy would accentuate the New Year's celebration.

A small, young lamb would be prepared – one for each family unless the family was too small. In that case, two families could join together in order to have sufficient supply. The amount would be enough for all to be filled but none would be left over – all would be consumed.

Prior to the choosing, this would simply be *"a"* lamb from the flock. The choice would be one that was without blemish. It was to be perfect in every aspect. Once chosen as *"a"* lamb, it would become *"the"* lamb. The lamb of choice was taken from the flock, being the best, and all others would be refused.

For fourteen days *"the"* lamb was watched, cared for, and made a part of the family. At the end of that time, *"the"* lamb was to become *"your"* lamb. Although, while in the flock it was just another of many, when chosen it became personal.

The blood represented the life that must be given in order to supply physical needs of the body. It was applied to the doorposts and lintels so that it ran down into the bottom of the doorway. That blood had protected the life of the first-born and provided physical salvation from death for all who were inside the door. Those who believed and made the lamb their personal lamb were also protected spiritually from eternal death.

The body was eaten (taken in) to provide life for those who participated. A life was sacrificed so that the believers could live.

When Jesus celebrated the Passover with His disciples, He told them to eat the bread and drink the wine (*Matthew 26.26-29*) remembering that it represented His body and His blood. This was radical to the disciples because, while they were reminded of a wooly lamb, Jesus wanted them to remember Him. While they had been taught to remember a physical deliverance from slavery in Egypt, Jesus wanted them to be reminded of His sacrifice of His own body for the deliverance from the bondage of sin. The Lord's Table was instituted so that all believers in Jesus Christ as Savior (the New Testament Church) would have a personal, experiential illustration of that deliverance.

Some today make much of the *"elements"* of the Supper, but the emphasis should always be placed squarely on the Lamb. When Jesus first stepped onto the scene for ministry, John the Baptist declared, *"Behold the Lamb of God which taketh away the sins of the world." (John 1.29)* Jesus commanded that the Lord's Table, which superseded the Passover, was to be done in remembrance of Him (*Luke 22.19*) and should be done often until He returns (*I Corinthians 11.26*).

Jesus is the fulfillment of the type set forth by the lamb in *Exodus 12*. He has been slain. His blood has been shed. He was selected by God Himself in eternity past for this purpose (*Acts 2.23; Revelation 13.8*). But although this Lamb is both *"a"* Lamb and *"the"* Lamb, He must also be *"your"* Lamb. He has already met the price for the sins of the world by making a sufficient payment, but His blood will not save until He is your personal Lamb.

Eat My Dust! Isaiah 65.25

"The wolf and the lamb shall feed together, and the lion shall eat straw like the bullock: and dust *shall be* the serpent's meat. They shall not hurt nor destroy in all my holy mountain, saith the LORD." (Isaiah 65.25)

It seems that no one takes a neutral position when it comes to snakes. Many people are intrigued by them while others are horrified by them. Some see them as low crawling creatures that rid the earth of even lesser desired creatures such as bugs and rodents. The snake has been studied for its fluid movements and even for healing properties allegedly attributed to its venom. One thing for certain is that, while I have seen people stop their cars to help a kitten, I have never seen anyone stop to nurse a snake back to health.

King Solomon in all his wisdom said that he was fascinated by the snake's ability to move on a rock (*Proverbs 30.19*). Even the Israelites, after having been delivered from the venomous creatures in the wilderness used the brazen serpent in their activities of worship seemingly as an idol. Because of the worship attributed to this serpent, King Hezekiah had it destroyed along with other paraphernalia connected with idolatry (*II Kings 18.4*).

Whether you love or loathe the snake, you must admit that it has some qualities that capture your attention. In the Garden of Eden, prior to the Fall, and when the first couple was innocent and had no reason to fear the serpent or any other creature; Satan used this creature to entice the pair into forsaking God.

The Bible uses the Hebrew word **nachash** to speak of the snake which suggests a hissing sound. Evidently the words spoken by this first tempter were different from the clear and plain words spoken by God. God has never hissed His message and has never been One to speak in a subtle (**arum** – *"crafty or cunning"*) fashion. His word has always been easy to understand for those who follow His direction. The problem with most Christians is not that God's Word is not clear but that we do not obey what we already know.

This serpent was special in the sense that it was being led by Satan to seduce Adam and Eve. Because of his charismatic personality, Eve followed him and so did Adam who was with her during the temptation (*Genesis 3.6 – "with her"*). From that time Satan has been related metaphysically with the snake. Often in Scripture he is called *"the serpent."*

Once Adam and Eve had disobeyed God and were confronted about their wrong, God pronounced judgment. The judgment upon Eve was multiplied sorrow and pain in child birth. To Adam the judgment consisted of a curse of the ground from which he came. In both of these, we can clearly see God's mercy and grace because the woman was placed under her husband's protection (*"desire"* and *"rule"* speak of Adam's responsibility to protect her from further deceit, *I Timothy 2.14*) while the man's work was to be toilsome. In effect, Adam would not reap and enjoy freely from the land but would be inclined to call upon God for help. This was a deterrent for Adam that hindered him from worshipping the land. In all of this, God was making it easier for Adam and Eve to approach Him rather than to flee to another god.

The curse on the serpent is another situation altogether. In approach to both the man and the woman, God questioned them, allowing them opportunity to repent and be reconciled. When God confronted the serpent, He did not ask but said, *"Because thou hast done this" (Genesis 3.14)*. There was no room for repentance or reconciliation.

Satan, in the guise of the serpent, was cursed (**arar** – *"inflict with a curse," "bind with a spell," or "to hem in with obstacles"*). **Arar** suggests that the one being cursed is powerless to resist. The blindness (*Jude 6*) that Satan finds himself in today renders him helpless to resist the power of God. Just as snakes today hide and sneak, so Satan must slither in the darkness and shrink when discovered.

His curse was to be so bitter that it would separate him from all other animals, from man, and from God. Because of this sin, all creation was under the curse due to the fact that all need the earth for survival, but the serpent would be so low to the ground that every meal – every mouthful – would be tainted with the earth.

The hope of mankind lies in the fact that, in the future, God will remove the curse from the earth. Today animals prey upon weaker animals. Mankind must tame wild animals or become part of the food chain. During the Millennial Kingdom of Christ, this curse will be ended. The wolf and lamb will be at peace with each other and the serpent's sting will be gone *(Isaiah 11.6-8)*.

One fascinating thought concerning the serpent during the Millennium is that even though it will be innocuous and not feared, the serpent will still be under God's curse *(Isaiah 65.25)*. The old song reminds us that *"There will be peace in the valley,"* but none for the serpent. The blindness that has chained Satan will continue through the end of time as he seeks souls for his kingdom. He will not, yea cannot, repent and turn to God.

The hope of the human race is not found in the earth although many worship it and use it to achieve their goals. The hope of humanity is not in conquering the land or in building empires. The hope of the world is Jesus Christ. Only as individuals submit to His authority and turn their hearts away from the world will there be peace.

If you have been looking for peace, look to the Savior – His blood cleanses from all sin and gives you peace with God.

Bucket Toters, Acts 6

"Then the twelve called the multitude of the disciples *unto them,* and said, It is not reason that we should leave the word of God, and serve tables. Wherefore, brethren, look ye out among you seven men of honest report, full of the Holy Ghost and wisdom, whom we may appoint over this business." (Acts 6.2, 3)

Early in my ministry as a young pastor, I found myself working with older men as deacons. Since I was of the ripe old age of 24, when I became a pastor, more than half of the entire church was older than me. At times the idea of training more mature men for the work of a deacon was humbling at best. On one particular occasion, as I tried to explain the complementary roles of deacon and pastor, one venerable deacon said, "Pastor, the way you talk we ain't nothing more than a bunch of bucket toters!"

I have thought about that quite often and there is much wisdom in a statement meant to check a young pastor against assuming a position that had for years been held by the "board."

One of the most basic concepts that governs the unity and operation of the local church is that each local congregation is a visible body of the Lord Jesus Christ. Each local assembly is called in Scripture to be autonomous and therefore has within it all talent and leadership necessary to do the ministry that God has called it to do. Drawing on outside resources such as evangelists, missionaries, literature, and such should not be overlooked, but the leadership within the body, when following God's plan and doing God's will can bring about a dynamic ministry.

Acts 6 delineates the work of the deacons and pastor by addressing the need that had been presented. Many churches today add ministries or programs just because others are doing the same thing. One of the blessings that our religious liberty affords is the diversity of styles of worship. No two places of worship are exactly alike; however, the leadership within the church must follow certain prescribed guidelines so that the body does not slide into error.

The problem that had arisen in *Acts 6* gave to the early church a wonderful opportunity to show to the world how a spiritual body operates in the physical realm. Some of the members were being neglected by the Apostles (the first church pastors) and the world began to think ill of the **Way**. Something needed to be done. The Apostles were being stretched too thin. The early church needed some bucket toters.

Before anyone becomes too offended, remember that without bucket toters, the fire burns the building. Without bucket toters, the thirsty perish for want of water. Without bucket toters, the sinking boat has no one to bail out the water. Without bucket toters, the levees break and the city is swamped.

The relationship that pastors and deacons have with the Lord is the same (or at least should be). Each should be desperately in love with their Lord and Savior and should desire more than anything else to do exactly what is God's desire for them. The relationship that pastors and deacons have with each other and all other church members should be the same – each are related as family by the blood of Christ.

Although the relationship in both situations is the same, the operation and application are different. The deacons were chosen to do the physical work of the ministry. In this situation, the deacons were chosen to ease the burden of the pastor concerning visitation and physical ministry. For some reason today the pastor has reassumed the role of visitation and most church members are offended if the pastor does not stop by from time to time or at least once a day when sick. Some pastors have even assumed the work of mowing grass and repairing leaky roofs for members. This tremendous work of the ministry was given specifically to the deacons.

As you read *Acts 6*, you will find that it was the responsibility of the deacons to visit and the responsibility of the pastors to study and pray – ministering the Word of Life. A church that does not make it easy for the pastor to spend much time in prayer and in the Word will never realize more than a superficial pulpit and teaching ministry. That church will run on left-over orts or sugar-coated drops while there is a feast available. While the church member wants to "see" the pastor, the pastor needs to "see" God.

The work of the deacon is vital to a Spirit-filled and vibrantly alive church. Notice again in *Acts 6.7* how when the pastors were allowed to meet with God in order to prepare the feast of God's Word, the church grew in wisdom, knowledge, and in numbers. And, notice how it grew – it was fervent.

Any organization with the right promotional materials can increase in numbers, but a healthy spiritual body is necessary for a body to properly represent Christ. Church members should utilize the church deacons in the physical ministry of the church. The pastors should leave the physical ministry in the hands of the Spirit-filled deacons. The deacons should serve in the areas to which they have been called that will allow the pastors the freedom to prepare a healthy and fresh meal for the family.

Bucket toters? In the Church of our Savior, we are all bucket toters. We need to be especially careful of is that we tote our bucket and not get in the way of others who are trying to tote theirs. When this becomes a reality, each member can take notice of how the Spirit of God will build the body – putting spiritual muscles on with power to spare.

Do Babies Go to Heaven? II Samuel 12.23

"But now he is dead, wherefore should I fast? can I bring him back again? I shall go to him, but he shall not return to me." (II Samuel 12.23)

Much speculation has been offered about the subject of a child after death. On the Calvinistic side of the debate, the opinion is that since grownups are predestined to either heaven or hell at death by God's election, then babies would fall into the same situation. Because of that no one can know whether a baby is predestined to go to heaven or predestined to go to hell. Of course the liberal scholar does not believe in the existence of a literal hell so this question presents no problem for him.

While I must admit that there is very little in Scripture that addresses anything concerning the eternal destiny of babies, it is not completely silent either. There are at least two thoughts that we must consider.

In the sin of Adam and Eve, it is true that, since Adam was the federal head of the entire human race, when he sinned he passed the sinful nature on to all of this family (*Romans 5.12*). The fact is, however, that even though all are under the curse of a sinful nature, no one receives eternal damnation for something someone else (including Adam) has done. Condemnation to hell is determined by personal guiltiness for sin.

When Jesus Christ died on the cross and shed His royal, sufficient, and holy blood, it was valuable enough to pay the price for all of mankind's sin and not just an elect few (*John 1.29*). In order to make the Bible say that Jesus died only for the elect takes some special interpretive and exegetical calisthenics. Because Christ died for the sins of the world, no one will be in hell because of a sin nature; but, I must hasten to say that freedom from penalty imposed against a sin nature is not enough for anyone to gain entrance into heaven either. In order to gain entrance into God's eternity, one must believe on the Lord Jesus Christ (*Romans 10.9, 10*). Just as no one goes to hell because of Adam's sin so no one goes to heaven without a blood sacrifice.

The blood sacrifice is sufficient for all (there is enough to reach all who come by faith), but it is only efficient (works to achieve the desired result) only for those who have the blood applied to their lives. This presupposes the act of believing or not believing. Those who know to make a decision are expected to do so to the saving of their eternal soul (*John 1.12*). By believing, the blood is efficient and cleanses from all sin – not only the sin nature (*I John 1.7* – walking in the light can only be accomplished by someone who believes).

Since a baby is too young to make a decision for or against Christ, we must realize that they have not rejected the Savior and that the sin of Adam will not cause them to go to hell; however, they have not believed unto salvation either. Based upon biblical principles and in nearly every civilization, nation, and group there is the concept of majority and minority ages. Prior to coming to a majority age, a child is not held accountable for his legal (or illegal) actions. The age of majority is arrived at on different ages in different cultures, but until that time someone else is responsible for the child's decisions. Spiritually, since Jesus Christ has paid the price for sin (the redemption price), the young who are unable to make that decision (because of age) fall under the authority of the One who is responsible – Jesus Christ.

One dynamic example from Scripture is found in *II Samuel 12*. While it is not my intention to go deeply into the sinful reasons that David and his son were here confronted with death, we should notice the fact that the child was dying in judgment on David's sin (*II Samuel 12.14*). This son that was conceived in sin was dying. He had nothing to do with the act of sin and was obviously too young to have chosen to be a follower of Jehovah.

Under the authority of God's Spirit, David stated very clearly that his son would not return to him but that he would one day join the son where he was. Since David was a man after God's own heart, the sweet psalmist of Israel, and the shepherd of God's people, it is not far reaching to acknowledge that David was in fact a believer. If he was to join his son, it must have been in God's presence. To say that David knew his son was "predestined" to heaven and not to hell would be laying into the hands of a mere mortal that which is reserved only for God.

Since David was not divine, he simply spoke what he knew to be true. He would go to his baby boy one day in a place where God dwells. All things considered, it is safe to say that any who have not reached a spiritual age of majority (some call this the age of accountability) are kept by the blood of Christ – after all *"will not the judge of all the earth do right?" (Genesis 18.24)*

Neglect Your Salvation? Hebrews 2.1-4

"How shall we escape, if we neglect so great salvation; which at the first began to be spoken by the Lord, and was confirmed unto us by them that heard *him;"* (Hebrews 2.3)

Much controversy has surrounded this passage of Scripture because of a lack of understanding. Some have suggested that certainly it must refer to the act of salvation in its initiation while others maintain that it must refer to the possibility of losing one's salvation. In order to understand the application the first concern must be to understand the context.

The context is not unlike that of the *Epistle to the Ephesians* where we must interpret the entire content with the knowledge that both books were written to people who were already believers. A major difference between the two books is that while *Ephesians* was written to teach believers from many backgrounds; Hebrews was written specifically to Jewish believers. *Hebrews 1.3* supports this teaching by referring to the readers as those who were purged from their sins. The word *purged* means that Christ had actively cleansed and purified them. A description of personal salvation could not be more succinctly portrayed.

This fact puts the weight of interpretation into the laps of those who believe *Hebrews 2* addresses the redeemed. Since it refers to the redeemed, we must come to an understanding of what is meant by the idea of letting something slip.

The slipping is a result of not giving the more earnest heed. That phrase indicates the listening of someone who waits with great expectancy. Picture, if you will, a six-year old boy whose father has been away and whose mother has told him that his Dad would soon be home with a surprise. At the expected time the young boy's mind is filled with anticipation as he asks his mother many times "When will Dad be home?" The boy is so insistent that this mother wearies of his questioning.

Finally, after what seems to be a lifetime, the father arrives and the boy leaps from what he is doing and into his father's arms. His senses are keenly alert while he inspects his father – looking for his surprise. That is *"giving the more earnest heed."*

It is essential that, as Christians, we attend carefully to the things of God or we will grow cold and lapse into neglect. A shop owner never needs to cheat on taxes or embezzle money in order to fail. A patient who has a curable yet deadly disease needs not to slit his wrists in order for death to overtake him. A farmer needs not to sow weeds or to put a fire to his crop in order to have no harvest. In each case, all that is needed is to do nothing.

Since I was born, raised, and lived all of my life in the South, I feel qualified to make a Southern comment about wealth. Some believe that the true test of wealth in the South is determined by how many vehicles are in the back yard on blocks. But those cars were not always on blocks. When they were put on the blocks, they were in better shape than they are today. What happened? Neglect!

Neglect causes us to lose sight of the beauty of a daily relationship with our Lord. Neglect dulls the spiritual senses so that Bible study, church attendance, and other related activities begin to pale beside ballgames and other worldly activities. Neglect cools godly friendships and alienates prayer warriors thereby weakening and often causing spiritual impotence in once ardent defenders of the faith.

Before proper adjustments can be made, neglect will lead to transgression and disobedience because the fear of reprisal will be gone. The word *transgression* means to "trespass knowingly" and the word *disobedience* means to "omit doing something that should be done."

Most Christians have justified driving 75 mph in a 70 mph zone by saying, "If I do the speed limit, someone will run over me," or "I know the law is 70, but no one will write me a ticket for going five mph over the limit." Neglect causes us to slip into transgression which by definition is premeditated sin. After all, the speed limit limits the upper range of speed and not the lower. Lest we consider that to be trivial, we must remember that it is the little foxes that spoil the vines (*Song of Solomon 2.15*). That kind of reasoning is proof positive that something has slipped. It must have been the type thinking that Adam and Eve did in the Garden of Eden – it was just a little piece of fruit.

On the other side of the argument is the idea of disobedience. Disobedience is not doing what we know we should. For example, I have always been mystified by how many Christians join churches, knowing the times of the services, and then only attend on Sunday morning or on special Holy Days. One Easter Sunday morning as I greeted the congregation as they were leaving, one of the "holly and lily" crowd (Easter and Christmas attenders) told me that I preach the same sermon every time they come.

What the attender said was probably true because it seems proper to preach about the resurrected Christ on Easter and that was the last time he had attended. When people join a church is it possible that they are truly not aware that the Church meets each Sunday and most meet for Sunday school, Sunday evening, and in the middle of the week for prayer and Bible study? Does the call of the lake or the mountains overshadow the call of responsibility to one's appointed place on Sunday? (*Hebrews 10.25*) Justification of missed church because of lesser important activities is being neglectful and not taking heed to what is important. By the way, there are very few things more important than *"exhorting one another."* If there is a question of planning, I would venture to say that the church was there first – before baseball, a cabin in the mountains, and even grandmother.

Neglecting our personal relationship with Christ, and other Christians, causes us to slip into apathy and apathetic Christians have a tendency to justify many things that should not even be considered. We should return to our childhood as we wait eagerly for a surprise from our loving Heavenly Father. He will not disappoint you.

What Holds the World Together? Colossians 1.16, 17

"For by him were all things created, that are in heaven, and that are in earth, visible and invisible, whether *they be* thrones, or dominions, or principalities, or powers: all things were created by him, and for him: And he is before all things, and by him all things consist." (Colossians 1.16, 17)

In a day when people's hearts shrink with fear and concern because of reports of coming disasters caused by global warming, tsunamis, earthquakes, and impending collisions with meteorites, the Christian can rest assured that all is still being controlled by our Creator. Early on, God promised that seasons and times would continue until He chose otherwise (*Genesis 8.22*). In spite of man's efforts at self-destruction and second guessing God, man can do nothing to thwart God's plan.

Just prior to Jesus' death and departure from the earth He gave promise of a coming Comforter (*John 14.16-18*). The Comforter promised was to be Another of the same kind – He too, is God. The Comforter would be the One who would hold the world together and be the indwelling Spirit of Christ for the believer.

Although those are great and wonderful thoughts, it gets better. When Paul was writing words of comfort to the Thessalonian believers who thought they had missed the Lord's return, he explained that the Lord would not return until the man of sin had been revealed. The man of sin could not be revealed until the Restrainer was removed (*II Thessalonians 2.7*). The word *"letteth"* in the King James Version is a usage that is somewhat unclear because the Greek word **katecho** means *"to hold fast, restrain, hold down, or suppress."* I would recommend that you read the entire epistle of *II Thessalonians* in order to have the context of the passage.

What Paul is saying requires us to understand that the only reason that Satan does not have complete control of the world and the reason total world-wide destruction has not yet happened is because the Holy

Spirit is not allowing it to happen. That fact, too, gives the believer comfort and confidence. The world will not and cannot end through a natural disaster or a nuclear holocaust so long as the Comforter is at work. Another point of comfort for the believer is the fact that this opportunity will follow the removal of the living believers and the dead in Christ from the earth (*I Thessalonians 4.13-18*).

A bit of a twist in understanding comes when we compare Scripture with Scripture. Because of the great soul harvest during the Tribulation Period (*Revelation 7.9*), and the fact that the Holy Spirit as God is omnipresent (everywhere at all times); He could not be completely removed from the earth at anytime. What that means is that God's Spirit is present even during the darkest days of the Great Tribulation and will still work in hearts drawing them toward salvation since no one can be saved apart from the Spirit's influence. To further prove that, one only needs to study the context of *Revelation 7.9*. There the Bible says that during this time of great world distress there will be a multitude from every people group on the earth that will be saved. That multitude must be enormous since it cannot be numbered, but the great army of 200 million can (*Revelation 9.16*).

A detailed description of what is stated in *II Thessalonians 2.7* was revealed to John while on the Island of Patmos in *Revelation 6*. Since the Holy Spirit is Christ's seal on the believers (*Ephesians 1.13; 4.30*), and since the Spirit is the One who today holds down evil; it is not a far stretch to recognize the seals on the scroll to be the Holy Spirit. In *Revelation 5* the only One found to be worthy to remove the seals was the Lamb because He was the One who set the seals in place.

As the Savior removes the Seals, He does not remove the presence of His Spirit but removes the protection offered to the unsaved world by the restraining effects of that Spirit. One by one the effective and specific protections applied to the world will be removed. World-wide famine that has been avoided will escalate. Death and disease will become pandemic in scope. The comets and meteorites that once missed the earth will then find their target. Man will truly be on his own against the forces of nature that have been groaning under the pressure of sin since it was introduced by our father and mother in the Garden of Eden (*Romans 8.22*). That groaning will turn into full-grown birth pains as evil emerges in the person of the Anti-christ.

The Holy Spirit will be removed bit by bit – seal by seal – until the human race will be completely left to its own devices. *Colossians 1.17* comforts the believing heart with the assurance that it is not a matter of human effort or human intelligence upon which the future of the world rests. The earth continues because the time of its demise, as determined by the Almighty, has not yet come. Only the Father knows the time and it can only occur after the Holy Spirit removes His protection. Until that time, the believer can rest assured that God is still on the throne and still in control.

Rusty Gold and Silver? James 5.3

"Your gold and silver is cankered; and the rust of them shall be a witness against you, and shall eat your flesh as it were fire. Ye have heaped treasure together for the last days." (James 5.3)

There are some things that are burned indelibly into your brain, and even though the date may have been long forgotten, the memory is clear. Such is the case of a memory about my first ring. It was lying on the ground just outside a game booth at the county fair. Since it had been trampled into the ground, only a portion was showing.

As I uncovered my newly found treasure, I convinced myself that it was gold and slipped it onto my finger. When I returned home I showed it to my parents – declaring its great value. They only smiled. My brother had a different opinion. His comment was something like, "That's not gold. It'll turn your finger green." Of course I had the perfect retaliatory comment, "Oh yeah!" Within a couple of days, my brother's prediction proved to be true and I walked around with green on my finger and a disappointed spirit.

James emphasizes the comparison and contrast between faith and works throughout his epistle. He also gives practical lessons that deal with Christian living and relationships with people and things. Chapter five begins by giving practical lessons about true and false wealth.

God's Word never condemns people who are rich. Remember that Abraham, who was required to make the sacrifice of his only son, was wealthy beyond imagination. And Job, who was the wisest of all the sages in the east, was also extremely wealthy.

Some read the Bible and say money is the root of all evil, but the Bible actually says the *love* of money is the root of all evil (*I Timothy 6.10*). There are some rich people who are quite godly and some poor people who are quite – well, not so godly. The false claim that those who live by faith and are righteous should be entitled to wealth places an onus on the poor, godly Christian that the Bible never intended either. After all, our Lord owned even less than the foxes and birds (*Matthew 8.20*).

James is not addressing wealth and poverty but ill-gotten gain in which the recipient of the funds sees the money as giving him power and ability. He skimmed money from those that he had hired and refused to earn his own wages honorably. Because of that, his gold and silver he so highly treasures fall far short of satisfying his inner most longings.

It turns out that the gold and silver are not real and they have turned the wearer's finger green. God says for them to weep and howl because they have trusted in the wrong god. Their wealth will not only turn colors but will corrupt and be worthless in the time of real need.

Notice two special words that may have caught your attention as they did mine. The word *cankered* (**katiao**) means to be rusted out or completely corroded. A friend of mine who lives in Michigan owns an old, small-sized pickup truck that he uses to haul firewood. The truck runs great and carries the driver and payload well, but is very rusted because of salt from the winter roads. As a matter of fact, if you plan to lean on the fender, you had better pick the right spot or you may fall through. At one time the truck was showroom perfect, but the perfection came to ruin through corruption (rust).

The other word, *rust* (**ios**), indicates that rust is being formed on or emitted from the metals. Emitted gives the connotation of something being injected as venom is injected through the fangs of a poisonous snake. Metaphorically, it speaks of the result of being deceived into believing that wine, introduced into a body, has no effect; but *"at last it biteth like a serpent, and stingeth like and adder." (Proverbs 23.32)*

It matters not what is the sin. When it has gained its target, it spews venom that will poison the individual. Beyond that, the one corrupted by the false treasure will spew poisonous philosophy for the minds of others – thus drawing a catch of followers deluded by the same poison.

Those who are led by God's Spirit and who have a proper relationship with Jesus Christ will understand the value of true precious metals. The metals (one's life and works) will be continually purified by the fire of testing and will become more precious as time passes. Impure metals will simply become more corrupt with age. God tests to bring out the best in His children. That sure beats walking around with a green finger.

To Swear or Not to Swear, James 5.12

"But above all things, my brethren, swear not, neither by heaven, neither by the earth, neither by any other oath: but let your yea be yea; and *your* nay, nay; lest ye fall into condemnation." (James 5.12)

It seems that almost everyone has an opinion about what the Bible says concerning swearing – including me. Some use this verse as a biblical mandate against placing their hand on a Bible and promising to tell the truth, the whole truth, and nothing but the truth. Some have considered this to be an act of cursing with foul language rather than taking an oath. Still others have no idea what is being said or to what it applies.

As has become customary, we must consider both the context of this verse and the etymology (*"the study of the sources and development of words"*). The first considerations must come from the two words in question: *"swear"* and *"oath."*

The word *swear* (**omnuo**) means to take or to make an oath. Jesus Himself used it in *Matthew 5.34* when He forbade swearing by heaven or by earth. It is specifically distinguished from *cursing* in *Matthew 26.74* in the account of Peter's denial of our Lord. When he was approached concerning his relationship with Jesus as he warmed himself by the fire, he cursed and swore. Cursing, in this context, suggests the same as the Old Testament concept of cursing which means to bind with an oath by one having the power to accomplish the expressed oath.

Swearing in this context and from its intended meaning simply implies that someone has affirmed or promised to do something. By invoking heaven or earth, the one promising to do something is calling upon powers beyond his ability or authority. James, then, tells the speaker to invoke neither heaven nor earth – neither should he make promises backed by something out of his control.

The other word that must be considered is *oath* (**horkos**). *Oath* is not a synonym but does carry some similar qualities. While the word swear seems to offer the moon and stars by a promise; oath is a word that means to promise but with limitations. When Herodias' daughter danced before Herod, she pleased him and he swore (**omnuo**) by his kingdom to give her anything she wanted to the half of the kingdom (*Mark 6.23*). Once he had sworn, the oath limited his ability and power because he could do nothing except fulfill his duty.

Some have suggested that this verse was arbitrarily placed in this spot in James and has no connection with the surrounding verses. We must consider; however, that it comes hard on the heels of three illustrations that seem to be left hanging with little or no context if not coupled with the warning of *James 5.12*.

The first of the three illustrations is that of a husbandman – a farmer (*James 5.7*). The farmer must work diligently in preparing his land and then he must wait patiently for the harvest. While he is working and waiting, many factors must be considered such as rain, heat, cold, and other such elements. To a novice, the wait seems unbearable until the time for the harvest. To the seasoned farmer, the wait is all a part of the reality of farm life.

Quite often circumstances arise that test the farmer's character. Storms, draught, heat, and cold can destroy the crop. Some farmers are tempted, under the pressure, to invoke heaven and earth to come to their aid – promising much that later is reneged on in order to lend weight to their promises.   Prayer is vital in anyone's life, but to bind oneself under promises during times of stress is never wise. The tendency in this first illustration is to swear an oath in order to have a more profitable harvest. This is swearing while under extreme stress due to hard physical labor.

The second illustration concerns the prophets (*James 5.10*) who were faithful in proclaiming God's message. It is not difficult for a pastor, Sunday school teacher, youth pastor, or other Christian worker to despair at the lack of concern in the heart of those to whom he ministers. Two pastors were conversing several years ago when one said, "I'll sure be glad when summer is over and everyone has come home from their vacation at the beach. We live too near the coast." The other pastor, a venerable sage, said, "We don't live too near the beach. We simply don't live close enough to the Lord."

When I was in Bible College, I heard of many pastors who had made great promises to the church of just what he would do if his church met their attendance goal on a particular Sunday. Only two should suffice to show how ridiculous some of these oaths were.

The first pastor set a goal for attendance and set the date for the entire congregation to bring their visitors. On that Sunday, he was prepared to parachute off the church steeple if the goal was met. It was. He did and broke both of his legs because the chute did not have space to open properly.

Another pastor, not to be outdone, went through similar preparations except that he promised to sit on a block of ice if his church met their goal. If memory serves me correctly, the block of ice was a cube of approximately two feet in each direction. The pastor promised to sit on it until it melted. This church also met their goal. The pastor was limited by his oath and sat. At one point someone (most probably the pastor himself) realized that something was not right so they rushed him to the hospital to be treated for frostbite. (It really makes one wonder who is leading the church of the living God.)

Both men were attempting to *"bring them in"* but must not have thought through their proposals. They swore by something they had no right to swear by and then were limited by their oath. They were under stress to achieve results in the ministry to show that they were making a difference.

The third illustration refers to the patience of Job. He showed himself to be righteous and upright even under extreme personal loss and physical pain. Some have ridiculed Job for lashing out on occasion against his friends, but the Bible says he did not sin with his mouth or accuse God falsely. And, before any of us get too self-righteous, consider how you would react if all of your children, wealth, possessions, and personal dignity was taken from you in a single day.

Have you ever cried out to God in despair, promising Him great things if He would deliver you from a certain stressful situation? Maybe you promised to read your Bible, attend church, or go to a foreign mission field for that relief? Job was patient through all of that and never once swore or made an oath.

James 5.12 is the conclusion to these three situations. We should never make rash vows in times of stress – no matter whether it is related to work, ministry, or personal problems. Our relationship to our Lord should be such that we trust Him and are able to wait patiently on Him – without the need of trying to twist His arm with our promises. After all, does that type of coercion seem a bit childish?

All Tears Wiped Away, Revelation 21.4

"And God shall wipe away all tears from their eyes; and there shall be no more death, neither sorrow, nor crying, neither shall there be any more pain: for the former things are passed away." (Revelation 21.4)

Heaven, a place of everlasting bliss, is a subject that mortal minds have contemplated since the earliest times. For now, we must understand that when we are absent from the body we are immediately present with the Lord (*II Corinthians 5.6-8*). As an old song says, *"For where Jesus is, that will be heaven for me."* Even if that was all there is, that should prove enough to satisfy the most insatiable heart, but God promises more.

Without going into a long discourse on heaven itself, we should be quick to remember that heaven is God's throne room and eternity for the saved will be in the coming city from God that Christ is preparing – the New Jerusalem (*Revelation 21.2, 3; John 14.2*). The city will be built with its eternal inhabitants in mind. It would seem that it will be quite similar to the original design of the Garden of Eden. The garden and the coming city contain creature comforts that are beyond man's wildest comprehension.

The passage in question tells us that God will reside with His redeemed because His dwelling place will be there. We also know that wondrous blessings will abound. What is difficult to explain is the implication expressed in the thought of wiping away all tears from our eyes.

Some would suggest that God will simply erase memories so that all of the past will be forgotten. That raises many problems with interpretation since outside the city are all manner of wickedness (*Revelation 21.27; 22.15*), and those who have not overcome but are barred from the blessings of the city (*Revelation 21.8; 22.14*). It is also obvious that those within the city are allowed freedom of passage through the gates of the city to go out and come inside again (*Revelation 21.27*), and that the nations with their kings will have rite of passage as well (*Revelation 21.24-26*).

All of this raises the question about wiping away all tears. It seems, contrary to popular opinion, that, when the saved arrive in that New City, they will see the vile and wretched on the outside – possibly even hear the anguished cries of the eternally damned. In the story of the rich man and Lazarus (*Luke 16*), not only could the rich man see into Abraham's bosom (a picture of the saved person's eternal home), but Abraham could see the torment of the rich man in his lost condition. We can assume that Lazarus could also see.

While it is true that the rich man mourned over the future plight of his brothers; Abraham and Lazarus shed no tears for neither him nor his brothers. As a matter of fact, Abraham seemed to have little or no pity but said to him, *"They have Moses and the prophets; let them hear them."* *(Luke 16.29b)* Was Abraham cold hearted when he became immortal? Will the saints of God be void of feelings in eternity? I think not. So what then? How can the redeemed peer into the other side of the eternity, across the great gulf, and still have no tears?

It is common, even today, for us to comfort one another through especially stressful times by exhorting each other with the thoughts that God's ways are not our ways because they are so much beyond us. We also often note the fact that when we are united with Him, we shall know His purpose and see more clearly than ever before (*I Corinthians 13.12*) His great plan for our lives and for accomplishing His will in the world.

On December 19, 1998, our sweet Savior chose to call to Himself our fifteen year old daughter Mandy by means of an automobile accident. Mandy had played for a soloist to sing in her first wedding just two weeks prior. She had accompanied our church choir on the previous Sunday evening as we performed our Christmas cantata "Christmas at Home." A great blessing for me was when I was selected to sing one of the solo parts accompanied by my daughter. All seemed to be going our way. She was scheduled to graduate a year early from high school and had her college plans all made. What went wrong? Nothing!

Our ways are not God's ways and many times our plans are just that – our plans. We heard many comforting (and not so comforting) words from many well-meaning people, but the tears still came and at times, years later, still do. One day my tears will be dried because I will see her again, but that is only a small part. I will also understand why.

When we are in the presence of our Lord and Savior, who loves us more than we can imagine, we will understand. Now, we see through a dirty window only a glimpse of the wisdom of God (*I Corinthians 13.12*), but then we will understand God's holiness and justice. Now we have difficulties in understanding how a merciful God could allow good people (humanly speaking) to spend eternity in torment. Then, we shall know as we are known and will understand perfectly what God has been doing. Since we will have the understanding as God has, we shall know perfectly and there will be rejoicing because of God's wisdom and mercy and justice.

All tears will be gone forever because we will see clearly God's great love and how He has worked to accomplish His plan of redemption in the world.

Who Goes First? I Thessalonians 4.15, 16

"For this we say unto you by the word of the Lord, that we which are alive *and* remain unto the coming of the Lord shall not prevent them which are asleep. For the Lord himself shall descend from heaven with a shout, with the voice of the archangel, and with the trump of God: and the dead in Christ shall rise first." (I Thessalonians 4.15, 16)

One of the great hopes upon which believers lean is the promise of Jesus' return. Paul wrote to the Thessalonian believers to encourage them and to assure them that they had not missed this appointed exodus from the earth. There are certain things that must occur in conjunction with what is commonly called the Rapture of the Church.

In this passage, the Bible says *"we which are alive . . . shall not prevent them which are asleep" (I Thessalonians 4.15)*. The word *prevent* is used transitively and means that one precedes the other or one is anticipated because of the other. In other words, those believers who are alive at the Lord's coming will not go ahead of those who are already absent from the body, but our hope is anticipated by the fact of their resurrection.

A Bible teacher not long ago answered the question of "Why do the dead go first" by jokingly saying that the dead have six feet further to go. Someone else, in a more sober fashion, suggested that since they were already gone and it was their bodies that would be taken out of the grave, they needed to be first (especially since the rest of us are still in our bodies).

While the normal understanding among those who interpret Scripture literally is that the dead will leave first, that is not exactly what is said. The passage indicates that they will rise first but not precede those who are alive. The phrase *"caught up together with them"* expresses a theme that is everywhere in this context. The word *with* is the same that is used in *verse 14*. In both places it means *"together with"* which implies a nearer and a closer connection than simply being in the presence of someone.

Suppose that you and your best friend, while on a camping trip and sharing the same tent, have an argument. In spite of the misunderstanding you are forced to be with your friend for the next several days. You are with your friend but you are probably not enjoying the time as you could if there was no friction between the two of you. After a day or so the two of you see the error of your ways and patch things up. With mutual cooperation and understanding you can now enjoy fishing, hiking, boating, and just being together with each other.

The latter of these two expresses something of the idea of being *together with* the Lord and *together with* them in the clouds. God's Word promises that we will be like Him because we shall see Him as He is (*I John 3.2*); therefore, we shall be *together with* Him and them.

The idea that some must go first seems to miss the entire point. The point is that we will be together and the fact that the dead rise first simply allows those who are dead and those who are alive to meet the Lord in the air together at the same time. To be with all the saved of all ages together with our Lord at the same time is incredible indeed, but there seems to be an added blessing for those who are alive at His coming.

Acts 1.9 assures us that the Rapture and Return will have visible qualities. The Coming for the saints will be visible to the saved and the Coming to the earth will be visible to every eye on the planet (*Revelation 1.7*). As Jesus left, so shall He return. Since all of this is true and since we shall be together it is only consistent to assume that the living saved will witness the resurrection of all the dead in Christ

What an amazing prospect – in a moment, in the twinkling of an eye – when God gives the word and Christ gives the command; the archangel will give the call and the trumpet will sound. Just at that moment the graves of all the redeemed will be emptied and the *departed* will spring forth from their repositories to be joined with their spirit in the presence of all living saints and together we will meet our Lord in the air – and so shall we ever be with the Lord.

Guardian Angels? Matthew 18.10

"Take heed that ye despise not one of these little ones; for I say unto you, That in heaven their angels do always behold the face of my Father which is in heaven." (Matthew 18.10)

Much speculation has been made by many people concerning the activities of heaven's residents. Some of the speculation (hopefully based upon Scriptural evidence) has been presented in this volume. The writer of Hebrews indicates that there is a great cloud of witnesses that watches the affairs of the world (*Hebrews 12.1*). Other evidence of the ability of those in heaven to see, or at least in some fashion, to be aware of earth's activities, can be found in *Luke 15.10*.

Some have read that verse to say that the angels rejoice over sinners who repent – and they possibly do; but the verse says that there is rejoicing in the presence of the angels. This points to those who are there other than the angels and indicates the saved who are in Paradise (but that is a topic for another study).

The point of this is to simply show the fact that heaven is quite aware of activities on earth. While those who have preceded us are unable to affect events on earth, there are some who both observe and have some power to act with relationship to living people.

Some who are before God's throne of grace are not there for our good. For example, Satan is the accuser of the brethren (*Revelation 12.10*) and, at present, seems to have access into God's presence (*Job 1.6; 2.1*). You can rest assured that his presence before God is not for the purpose of fellowship. He is always up to no good and can see activities on earth and affect events as God permits.

It should give us some comfort to realize that Satan cannot attack every Christian personally so he most probably focuses his personal attention on people who are big targets with greater influence than an average saint. But, before you get too comfortable, Satan has help. Remember that he has ranks of followers that carry out his orders through well organized efforts.

Even though most have no difficulty in accepting the reality of the interference caused by Satan and his forces, those same people would relegate the idea of guardian angels to a mother's bedtime story. A careful study of Scripture would indicate that there is a great war being fought in a realm beyond our ability to see.

Do you remember the story of Elisha and his servant when they were surrounded by enemy forces? (*II Kings 6*) Elisha sat so calmly that his servant seemed to become agitated by his lack of concern. When the young man confronted Elisha, he responded by praying, *"Lord, I pray thee, open his eyes, that he may see." (II Kings 6.17)* As an answer, the young man's eyes were opened so that he could see the Lord's hosts standing guard over them. Elisha had not invoked heavenly activity – it was already involved.The angels of God are alert to His voice and ready to minister to the saints. That brings us to our verse at hand and to the subject of guardian angels. *Matthew 18.10* warns against despising (*"to hold in contempt or to think lightly of"*) the little ones which, in this context, refers to children. Jesus goes on to say, *"That in heaven their angels do always behold the face of my Father which is in heaven."*

To behold the Father's face means that they have the focused attention of the Father and the Father has their focused attention. They are literally eagerly awaiting the Father's commands.

Most of the times we think of guardian angels as the great protectors of two year olds – after all, two year olds need a little extra care.

Shortly after moving to the Summerville (SC) area, our middle daughter (then four years old) was put into the care of a dear, godly lady during the summer months. As part of the summer activities, our care-giver took her wards to a county park filled with playground equipment. I can still remember vividly our meeting that afternoon when I went to pick up our little darling. The care-giver informed me that our daughter, who was only out of her sight for a second, made her way to the top of the swing set and was going hand-over-hand across the support beam (about ten feet above the ground). She said, "Her guardian angel must have been watching over her."

That was probably quite true, but the context here indicates special attention given to those who would abuse, neglect, or think lightly of children. Little children are special to our Lord. In the middle of a very busy day, while teaching and ministering to multitudes, our Lord stopped what He was doing and encouraged the little children to come to Him (*Matthew 19.14*)

Although we would never think of abusing or neglecting our children, or the children in our neighborhood, we often think lightly of them. Last Sunday, did you take your little ones to a church that teaches and preaches the Bible as the Word of God? If you did, did you fill all of your empty car seats with little ones from your neighborhood?

Remember that each little one has an angel who always beholds the face of the Father and can act on behalf of that little one. It would be nice to think that while the Devil is accusing us, some little one's angel is at the same time giving a good report of our attention to and care for them.

Collecting Hoary Heads, Proverbs 16.31

"The hoary head *is* a crown of glory, *if* it be found in the way of righteousness." (Proverbs 16.31)

In the South, it is not uncommon for people to put much stock in their collecting of things. Housewives collect plates, pots, and recipes. Some collect baseball cards and other memorabilia. One gentleman in my church who is a farmer collects farm equipment. Recently he collected his fourth tractor but very quickly admitted to promising his wife that he would buy no more unless he first ridded himself of at least one from his collection.

My wife has a collection of Precious Moments figurines that can almost analog the history of our family. While she has bought none of them personally, they have appeared as gifts from people (including myself) for special occasions until her collection now numbers more than one hundred.

Within the past twenty years or so, my collection of mugs has increased to the point of out-growing any spare shelf space in my study (along with a couple of mug trees made specifically to display them). I do not remember ever purchasing more than a couple of them, but it seems that kind folks have offered them as gifts of thoughtfulness over the years. Most of them mark special people and moments of time so that when I look around my study, I am reminded of God's goodness and grace in surrounding me with wonderful friends who love the same Savior that I do.

One collection that introduces me to very special people, most of whom I have never met, is my library. The first books that were to become friends came into my possession while in high school. Commentaries, biographies, theological studies, collections of sermons, and even fiction fill shelves (that otherwise would probably display mugs) from wall-to-wall and number about five thousand. For many years I would go to the books for sermon preparation and inspiration while looking for wisdom beyond my years of experience. Very few times was I disappointed as I visited with the authors' works and read marvelous studies and sermons from such noted men as A. W. Tozier, Oliver B. Greene, Vance Havner, Lehman Strauss, and Lee Roberson.

All of these godly men are now with our Lord – some I have had the privilege of meeting and hearing in person, but all of them I have learned to love and appreciate because of their godly testimony and spirit-filled wisdom. As I get older, most of my visits with these *"hoary heads"* are for personal reason – many times just visiting with old friends.

The term *"hoary heads"* refers to maturity that quite often is marked by gray hair. As a matter of fact, the term *"hoary"* means gray or white. The Bible says, *"The hoary head is a crown of glory, if it be found in the way of righteousness." (Proverbs 16.33)* Just to have a head full of gray hair does not necessarily indicate that a person is full of wisdom. Wisdom comes from a life spent walking in the ways of righteousness. The author of Proverbs gives instructions for the gaining of collections that matter. *"Wisdom is the principal thing; therefore get wisdom: and with all thy getting (possessions or collections) get understanding." (Proverbs 4.7)*

I have learned over the years that not everyone who is filled with wisdom writes books and, too, that some who write books do not necessarily possess wisdom. Some of the most godly and wisest men that I have known are those who populate local churches – those who have walked faithfully in a small congregation, following our Lord and His will. Young pastors could learn much from them – especially things that deal more with culture than theology. Mistakes can often be avoided by making some of these *hoary heads* your counselors and friends.

One of the greatest blessings in life is when young people (or not so young people) make it a point to collect *hoary heads*. In other words, God has given to this world and to His Church many who by reason of age and their walk in righteousness have obtained knowledge and wisdom.

In a day of fast-paced religious experiences that seems to always look for bigger, better, and faster; we should slow down a little and sit on an old-fashioned porch swing and enjoy the sweet fellowship that we have cultivated with our collection of *hoary heads*.

Vance Havner was once asked, after a long life of service for our Lord, what he would do differently in his ministry if he could change anything he chose. He responded by saying, "I'd do less." He went on to explain that so much of ministry seems to be done in a hurry and so few take time to enjoy the Lord of the work. We do the same thing with older folks in church. Often they are relegated to a back seat when their wisdom and fellowship should be cherished.

They are slower and their methods are not high-tech, but they have a life-time of walking with the Master. Maybe as we spend time walking with them we will gain valuable insight into what pleases our Lord and Savior. As you go on with your collections, be sure to collect the *hoary heads* that can help you gain wisdom and knowledge and can show you how to walk in righteousness. I would guess that they have as much time for you as you do for them.

Wings and Legs, Isaiah 40.31

"But they that wait upon the LORD shall renew *their* strength; they shall mount up with wings as eagles; they shall run, and not be weary; *and* they shall walk, and not faint." (Isaiah 40.31)

Have you ever known someone who seemed so busy that they accomplished very little? Many years ago, Dennis the Menace said, "The hurrier I go the behinder I get." Most people have felt that way at some time in life.

As I get older, I find that I need to pace myself or else some activities will last longer than I do. When in high school, I once ran the forty yard dash in 4.4 seconds. At the present time, I am simply happy to make it from the starting line to the finish line.

It is not necessarily a bad thing to slow down. At a walk, I can go forty yards now just as easily as I could when I was younger and I can do it as many times now as then. Along the way, there is just as much and sometimes more enjoyment than before and if a flower or bird appears along the path, I have time to stop and enjoy it.

Isaiah speaks of soaring, running, and walking. At first it would seem that the order is all wrong until one examines a bit closer. The preceding verse speaks of the young growing faint (*"exhausted or tired"*) and weary (*"to grow tired of working"*). Because of the fact that the ones in question act with their own strength, they faint and become weary and ultimately fall (*"stagger or stumble"*). The word fall is intensified and is rightly translated *"utterly fall."* In other words, the one who relies upon self apart from God is hopeless and helpless.

But, those who wait upon (*"to wait for, or hope for"*) the Lord will find strength beyond themselves. The root for this verb is **qawah** which indicates a twisting or winding of stands of a cord to make a rope – thus strengthening it and making it more reliable. Hope in one's self is feeble, at best, but hope in the Lord is a surety that allows us to work effectively without tiring ourselves.

A tremendous principle is shown here suggesting while youth may soar as eagles, they will accomplish little or nothing unless they are empowered by the Lord. Not only must the initial direction be established by God's design, but also the pace of the venture. *Amos 3.3* asks the question, *"Can two walk together except they be agreed?"* Walking together suggests several concepts that must mesh in order for the walk to be successful. 1) There must be a common starting point. 2) All who walk together must follow the same route. 3) Each walker must have a common destination with the other walkers. 4) All involved must walk at the same speed. 5) In order to have fellowship while walking, there must be a common topic for discussion.

For a Christian to soar when he should be walking is just as wrong as walking when he should be running.

Most often *Isaiah 40.31* is seen to express the steps of the young Christian who, at first, is soaring in his new found freedom and blessing in Christ. As he gets older in his spiritual life, his soaring settles into a run and eventually slows to a walk with age. That is most probably accurate, but we must remember that whether soaring, running, or walking, the believer who acts at the will of God will not tire. It is a matter of surrender not pace.

Many years ago during my first pastorate, a friend of mine, my father, and I decided to chop some firewood for an elderly lady of our church who heated with wood. Since Dad was older, I took him more for the fellowship than for the work he would provide. My friend and I were in our mid-twenties – Dad in his late fifties.

My father had learned to split logs that were six feet in length as a youth in Stokes County, North Carolina for heating tobacco barns that would cure the crop and for building split-rail fences. At the time I was completely unaware of Dad's skill and since Dad always moved at a determined pace, I assumed that he would work steady but not nearly as fast as my friend and I.

I began to saw down the trees (small black-jack oaks) and trim the limbs with a chain saw while my friend and Dad began splitting the pieces that were large enough to split. I could see they were doing a fine job keeping pace with my saw and, after an hour and a half or so, I felt we had enough sawed wood so I stopped sawing. As I looked at the two men, my friend (the younger) seemed to be "tuckered out" but my father had not seemed to have broken a sweat. As my friend stumbled, dragging his axe and feet, across the fallen brush, he pulled me aside and said, "Don't ever embarrass me like that again. Your Dad split two to my one and hasn't even tried very hard." So much for the strength of youth.

All that to say this – my father knew the "technique" for log-splitting. Neither my friend nor I did. I am certain we both worked harder, sweated more, and were more exhausted at the end of the day than Dad; but he knew the secret to success. It was Dwight L. Moody who said that when he was young he carried many buckets of water to the dying souls in the Lord's name. As he matured in his faith and understanding he began to see the supply of water was from the Holy Spirit and he needed it as much as the dying. With that came the understanding that it was the Holy Spirit doing the work so he could, in his later years say that the supply became a great river that carried him. The supply is always there, but sometimes we are so accustomed to doing things in our own strength and at our own speed that we neglect to fellowship with the Savior along the way. Because of that we tire early and give up when we should persevere.

No one can honestly question Mr. Moody's effectiveness for our Lord and no one can doubt the power of his ministry. The key was not in his busyness (busyness tends to wear down the worker), but in the fact that he had learned to wait on the Lord. When we learn the secret of doing in God's strength and will, the believer can soar with wings as eagles, run and not be weary, and walk and not faint because he will know when to soar, when to run, and when to walk. The trip will be as enjoyable as the arrival because we will be with our Lord along the way and in agreement with His will.

Was Jesus in Hell? Ephesians 4.9,10

"(Now that he ascended, what is it but that he also descended first into the lower parts of the earth? He that descended is the same also that ascended up far above all heavens, that he might fill all things.)" (Ephesians 4.9, 10)

Depending on which version you read, the Apostle's Creed may or may not include the phrase that says Jesus descended into hell. Both sides of that argument have been debated and some weight of evidence exists pointing to each conclusion.

One of the arguments for proposing Jesus' descent into hell is the idea that, in order to suffer for all men, that suffering must include the pangs of hell. In one Bible class in seminary, the professor explained that a mortal must suffer infinitely for his sin because he is finite but the infinite character of Jesus Christ would only require a short amount of time for the infinite to experience enough wrath to satisfy God's holy demands. How long was the requirement? No one seems to know, but this is an attempt to explain something that is not clearly taught in Scripture.

These writings are not intended to produce deep theological thoughts, but to provide an uncommon view of some common verses – to provoke readers to looking beyond truths that are simply parroted because they have not been thoroughly studied.

Many people who recite the Apostles' Creed never stop to think about the words and often are unaware of the significance of whether Jesus went to hell or not.

The Bible says, *"For thou wilt not leave my soul in hell; neither wilt thou suffer thine Holy One to see corruption" (Psalm 16.10).* The word **corruption (sahat)** indicates a pit, a ditch, a grave, or a hollow place. Most commonly **sahat** refers to the decay of the body but also has been applied to the pit of destruction from which the Lord's love and mercy saves *(Isaiah 38.17).* The noun form is used to denote Sheol (*"the abode of departed spirits" – Job 33.24; Ezekiel 28.8). Psalm 16.10* seems to state that the Lord Jesus Christ would not be placed into hell because He would not be allowed to see corruption. In opposition to the thought of corruption is the promise of everlasting joy (*Psalm 16.11*). These two expressions together suggest that life after physical death is indicated and that the Holy One would not suffer the second death.

So then, what about *Ephesians 4.9, 10*? It would seem perfectly clear that Paul is referencing Jesus' descent into hell. How could anyone read into this something else?

It is true that some have used this as a proof text to teach Christ both died and that He went to the dwelling place of disembodied spirits which is called Hades in the New Testament. Others have understood this instead to mean the lower parts of earth itself and not to a part of the earth's insides. The lower parts, then, are contrasted with the upper parts – above the clouds in the heavens from where Christ originally descended.

Psalm 139.15 says, *"My substance was not hid from thee, when I was made in secret, and curiously wrought in the lowest parts of the earth."* In the original creation, Adam was formed of the dust of the ground. Here, however, the Psalmist speaks of his own formation which occurred on planet earth and above ground. In either case, the lowest parts of the earth do not indicate a subterranean place, but the surface.

The point of *Ephesians 4.9, 10* is not to prove one way or another about the possibility of Jesus' descent or lack of descent into hell. Also, the point of this article is not to make a statement in proof of either position but to make a simple statement about personal Bible study. The true believer should be like the Berean believer who searched the Scriptures daily. Just because a preacher makes a statement loudly or bangs on the pulpit or makes it with great energy does not make it so, and just because you have heard it all of your life does not make it true.

God's Word has stood the test of time and has stood unchanged by skeptics and enemies of the cross of Christ; therefore, I am certain that it can handle the deep searching of someone who truly loves their Lord and Savior. The only thing that could happen to a person who engages in a deep study of God's Word and in spending much time with their Savior would be a change of heart and mind in the seeker. This is what God desires – fellowship with His children.

Satan is quite content with people who repeat platitudes – no matter how good they are – even when they contain truth. If they have become meaningless words, they do not have the power to change lives.

God desires us to know His Word because in knowing His Word we know Him (*II Timothy 2.15*). If you find this article unpalatable or reprehensible, take out your Bible, study it, and learn firsthand where Jesus went when His body was in the grave.

By the way, *Ephesians 4.9, 10* simply states the fact that in order for Jesus to be Savior He had to come to earth from heaven and then leave earth to return to heaven. Check it out.

Land o' Goshen, Genesis 45.10, 11

"And thou shalt dwell in the land of Goshen, and thou shalt be near unto me, thou, and thy children, and thy children's children, and thy flocks, and thy herds, and all that thou hast: And there will I nourish thee; for yet *there are* five years of famine; lest thou, and thy household, and all that thou hast, come to poverty." (Genesis 45.10, 11)

I suppose that the phrase "Land o' Goshen" could be considered a mild expletive but I cannot understand why. It is hardly ever used any longer and as I recall the only people that I ever heard use it were either my grandparents or someone on an old western movie. It seemed to have a variety of uses and applications but was normally used to express amazement over some surprising situation.

According to Scripture, the Land of Goshen was the land for which Joseph bargained with Pharaoh on behalf of his family when they moved to Egypt because of the great famine. The famine had rendered Egypt and Canaan impotent as the people vainly tried to provide for themselves.

Goshen was some of the best pasture land in all of Egypt. Pharaoh pastured his herds there and because of his great respect for Joseph, he agreed to allow the fledgling nation of Israel (numbering seventy souls) to settle there. Its choiceness was evident because it was also called the Land of Rameses.

Because of Pharaoh's respect for Joseph, he also asked Joseph to appoint some of his family members to be overseers of his herdsmen. Joseph's family soon settled in and became comfortable with their surroundings. Even Joseph's wife, Asenath (daughter of an Egyptian priest), was accepted as part of the seventy (*Genesis 46.20, 27*).

God gave His blessing to the occupation of this land by telling Jacob to go and, in time, Jacob's family would become a great nation. It did. It seems, however, that they over-stayed their welcome and Joseph's genius was forgotten. After many years the blessing of the Jewish population became a supposed threat so the new Pharaoh subjugated them into slavery.

There is, in this narrative, something that seems rather odd. Most Bible scholars agree that the Land of Goshen was in the northeastern part of Egypt bordered on the west by the Nile River, on the north by the Mediterranean Sea, and on the southeast by the Red Sea. That all fits because the Nile River would have provided water and it is believed that during those years the entire area was lush with pasture land.

If this is the case, it raises the question of why, when severely enslaved, did the Israelites stay in the land rather than packing up and stepping across the border into Canaan. In order to cross the Red Sea during their Exodus, the nation would need to go a considerable distance to the south prior to the crossing. It is evident from Scripture that they went across on dry land that was normally covered with water deep enough to drown the entire Egyptian military force upon its return. This, in itself, puts enough weight on Israel's path to put to rest the liberal's argument that the nation crossed in the shallows. Although from the liberal's perspective, this would make sense, they simply change the miracle of God's power from moving water to drowning the world's most formidable army in ankle deep water.

So then, why did they go the distance? There is the possibility that they did not have far to go. In the move to Egypt an assimilation of cultures had begun. Remember that Joseph's wife was the daughter of a priest and during their four hundred plus years in Egypt, there is little mention of God. Over the years Israel had become comfortable with much that Egypt had to offer. The leaders (elders) had located near Pharaoh's palace is evidenced by the events surrounding Moses' offers to and demands of Pharaoh – the elders seemed to be close at hand, even complaining of Moses' attempts to free God's people. In the wilderness, the Israelites expressed their longing for the fleshpots, leeks, and garlic of Egypt.

Although there was still distance between much of the population and Egypt's capital, the Israelites were mingled enough so that they could borrow from their *neighbors* – the Egyptians (*Exodus 11.2, 3*). The miracles of plagues that devastated Egypt seemed to be as much for the benefit of Israel as it was for Egypt. God used His awesome power to pry His people from their mingled relationships. (We should note the fact that God led them south in order to avoid immediate conflict with the Philistines, *Exodus 13.17.*)

Even though God has placed His children in the world, we must not become a part of the world. As many Israelites as there were in Egypt and as many years as they had to be a witness for the true God, there is little evidence that many were converted to the God of Israel.

The situation is similar today in our God blessed land. The Christian has become so much like the world that, for many, to think of the Rapture causes one's mind to think of possessions, friends, and relationships on earth and not of eternity with Christ. All that the world offers should be tools for the Christian in his quest for godliness but should never cause us to be comfortable in this world (*Matthew 6.33*).

Had God not intervened with Israel, they would have probably chosen to stay in Egypt as slaves. The Christian looks forward to God's intervention when He will split the sky with the sound of the trumpet to call His children home (*Thessalonians 4.13-18*). Our prayer should never be, "Lord just a few more leeks and garlic." It should ever be "Even so come, Lord Jesus."

Where is Grandma? Revelation 6.9-11

"And when he had opened the fifth seal, I saw under the altar the souls of them that were slain for the word of God, and for the testimony which they held: And they cried with a loud voice, saying, How long, O Lord, holy and true, dost thou not judge and avenge our blood on them that dwell on the earth? And white robes were given unto every one of them; and it was said unto them, that they should rest yet for a little season, until their fellow servants also and their brethren, that should be killed as they *were*, should be fulfilled." (Revelation 6.9-11)

So often we Christians talk about heaven and our planned trip there, but when we come to a need of expressing what we believe about it, we begin to falter and stammer. Sometimes our descriptions of Heaven lack enough information that it may, to some lost people, seem bland – after all, who would want to float in the clouds and play harps for all of eternity. That may get old after the first few millennia. When pressed for a description of Heaven, even some venerable older saints give descriptions that are akin to cartoon caricatures rather than well-defined, biblical answers.

A problem sometimes arises when the soul winner approaches an unbeliever and offers him heaven only to be asked the question concerning the nature of heaven. To tell a saint who has walked with his Savior for many years that he has the privilege of spending eternity with Christ is certainly a blessed thought; but to tell a lost person the same information may not be quite as appealing. His thoughts of heaven may take him to scenes of Sunday morning church (a place that may or may not be familiar) with a choir and a bunch of people in Sunday "go-to-meeting" clothes. Several years ago, I was attempting an explanation to an unbelieving friend of the great advantages of heaven and the dismal prospects of hell when he told me that he would rather spend his time alone in hell than to spend eternity with all the church folks singing, playing harps, and going to revival meetings all the time. It was obvious that I had done a rather poor job of explaining the benefits of heaven; but also obvious was his confusion concerning the vast gulf of difference between the two places.

The point is that there are many differing ideas about heaven – some bear accuracy to the facts while others offer neither resemblance of truth nor reality. *Revelation 6.9-11* speaks specifically of martyrs who are in heaven during the Tribulation Period. Even though this period of time will be filled with special events on the earth, there is no need to make one's existence in heaven anything other than what has been experienced from the beginning of the Church Age.

Several indicators point to specifics that will help the reader better understand what Heaven really is and what is there. In *Revelation 6.9*, the Bible explains that these martyrs are actually people who once lived on earth but have been relocated to heaven. They are *"just men made perfect" (Hebrews 12.23)*. Notice too, that they were remembered as having lived on earth because their testimony spoke volumes in their present existence. As a result, their heavenly existence simply continued on from this earthly existence. This also suggests that those in heaven will remember others and will be remembered by others because of their testimony from their earthly existence. This leads us to draw the conclusion that their personality and characteristics will also be a part of their person in Heaven.

Revelation 6.10 says that the martyrs *"called out,"* which suggests they were able to articulate their thoughts. The word interpreted *"cried"* **(krazo)** is the same word used of Jesus' cry from the cross during the three hours of darkness. Some have suggested that crying out indicates physical bodies or at least the ability to articulate thoughts. This thought agrees with the Apostle Paul when he made it clear that every believer will be *"clothed" (II Corinthians 5.2-4)*. In other words, the believer will always have some form or body – even in the intermediate state between earth and eternity (The intermediate state is the place we call heaven – where God is and where all saints who have left this world now live waiting for the New Heavens and the New Earth. *Revelation 21 & 22*)

Another indication that saints in heaven have bodies today is the mention of robes. Since the Bible nowhere indicates or vaguely suggests the possibility of ghosts, it is most unlikely that these robes would be draped over a bodiless spirit. If there was no body, the martyrs would at best appear to be ghost-like. Each of these martyrs, however, is a unique individual who has physical form and was in unity of desire and purpose with the others present at the altar.

The martyrs voiced their opinions in prayer to God asking Him to move quickly, which is, in essence, a prayer (and one that each Christian should pray often) – *"Even so come, Lord Jesus."* Their prayers were pure because, as we have been taught many times, prayer is not getting our will done in heaven, but getting God's will done on earth. Just think for a moment how powerful would be our prayer life if we could abandon ourselves of our sinful thoughts. These martyrs were not crying out in selfish desires but in perfect harmony with the Will of God.

They know what is happening on earth and care about people, events, and judgment. Heaven dwellers are not passively idling their time away; but, they pray (plead with God) and they learn (by asking questions they seek further knowledge). It would seem that the concerns for world events will not diminish when reaching heaven but will actually be heightened. The martyred will remember that they were murdered (and probably that they were tortured) in Christ's service and will not be satisfied until God judges His enemies and puts them under His feet.

Those in Heaven will no longer see through a glass darkly (*I Corinthians 13.12*), but will see clearly God's divine attributes (*...holy and true..., v. 10*). Clear vision and righteousness do not; however, indicate omniscience. The saints ask questions meaning they are still learning, but without the sin nature any longer, the learning will be easy. They will have no need to "cram" for a test. How can a statement be made concerning their learning? After all, when we get to Heaven, will we not know everything there is to know? The fact that the martyrs asked questions and received answers indicates that they knew more after the questions were answered. God's response (the new, added information) was that He will answer their prayers but they needed to wait a bit longer.

The martyrs seem to be free to ask any question they wish which would also indicate using their thought processes. They are not automatons, but are thinking, reasoning, and conscious souls. They are aware of each other's existence and actually have a close relationship with others who are there (*"fellow servants and brothers"*).

So then, what is Heaven like? It is essentially being in the presence of God, with our Savior, in a real place with other real people.

There, the curse of sin cannot penetrate and God's perfect love overshadows every relationship. It is not floating around the universe, but is a place – a real place – where the fountain of Jesus' blood flows and salvation's fellowship is unhindered. No evil thought or action can invade its borders and nothing can cause harm. Our bodies will be clothed with the garments of Christ's righteousness even as Adam and Eve were prior to their sin of unbelief.

In perfect harmony, we will fellowship (in person as did Moses on the mountain and John on the Isle of Patmos) with the King of all ages and with beloved saints (as the disciples on the Mount of Transfiguration experienced) of all ages.

Where is Grandma? If she believed in the Lord Jesus Christ and she is no longer living on earth then she is living in heaven – clothed in the righteousness of Christ and experiencing fellowship with the Savior and other saints who are there. She is calling on her Savior to bring this age to an end, to vindicate Himself by judging the world, and to reunite the saved on earth with the saved in Heaven. Where is Grandma? She is in a perfect place, with a perfect people, controlled by a perfect God.

Face to Face with God, Exodus 24.10

"And they saw the God of Israel: and *there was* under his feet as it were a paved work of a sapphire stone, and as it were the body of heaven in *his* clearness." (Exodus 24.10)

One specific difficulty the dispensational premillenialists (or any others who interpret Scripture literally) must answer is the question of the possibility of those who are evil gaining access to the presence of God. The argument is that since Christ died on the cross and paid the price for sin at a specific time in history, no one, prior to that point in time could go to heaven because sin was only covered by animal sacrifices and not cleansed by the blood of Christ.

The Old Testament, however, speaks often of those who found personal, face-to-face audiences with God. Abraham spoke with God face-to-face on at least two occasions concerning God's promise of a son who would become a great nation. God spoke with Moses on several occasions when plans were being made operative in the effort to free Israel from Egyptian bondage. After the Fall God sought out Adam and spoke to him in the Garden of Eden prior to the expulsion and outside the Garden of Eden following the expulsion. Many more illustrations are easily found for the earnest Bible student.

Two men take center stage in this unfolding drama who, not only saw God, but also walked with Him and went into His holy presence as a living, breathing person. On one special day Enoch walked with God all the way from his home to God's home – by-passing death. Elijah went out in a flurry as God sent His special couriers to take Elijah to his heavenly home. Many say these two men are exceptions to the rule, but in fact, they are examples of the rule. When God says things are either this way or that way, He means exactly what He says. He is no respecter of persons.

The sight of heaven is indeed a splendid vision. Other than what Jesus Himself reveals of the eternal New Heaven and New Earth (including the New Jerusalem), most of what we know of heaven deals with God's throne room. John wrote of it in *Revelation 4 & 5*. In it exists a menagerie of creatures including the seraphim Isaiah saw (*Isaiah*

6) and the twenty-four elders John saw (*Revelation 4*). Whether John was in the body or in the spirit (I believe he was both in body and spirit), he was in the throne room of God, and it bears a remarkable resemblance to the scene shown in *Exodus 24.10.*

Moses read to the people of Israel from the book of the covenant and all the people agreed to obey it. It seems plausible to assert that they promised to obey the letter as well as the spirit of the law. After the commitment, Moses offered a blood sacrifice, sprinkling half of the blood on the altar and the other half on the people. Then, Moses, Aaron, Nadab, Abihu, and seventy elders of Israel entered God's presence. They saw God. They saw Him in person; in a physical form (He had feet.). Twice we are told they saw God.

They saw the smoothly paved court of the throne room – paved with "worked" sapphire stone. It was such a beautiful sight that it appeared to be the essence (**esem** – "*body, bone, substance, self*") of heaven itself. The first time the term **esem** is used is in *Genesis 2.23* when Adam exclaimed "*This is now bone of my bone.*" God made Eve to be a part of Adam so that one was incomplete without the other. By application, the beauty and worth of heaven are a declaration of the great awesomeness of God and with all its beauty, it is worthless without God.

Were they in the body or in the spirit? *Exodus 24.11* says, "*. . . also they saw God, and did eat and drink.*" It seems obvious that they were in the presence of God in their bodies since they had physical food and drink. After the meal and the face-to-face meeting with God, Moses went further – to the top of the mountain – to commune with God. All of this speaks of the effulgent, resplendent glory of the great God of creation. Into that Moses went and stayed for forty days – into God's presence.

There seems to be too many illustrations of sinful men being in God's presence to simply ignore them, try to explain them away, or to suggest they are exceptions to the rule. It is much easier to compare Scripture with Scripture than to hold to misunderstood concepts of fallible man.

The key to understanding how sinful man could be in the presence of an all-holy God is mentioned in passing in *Revelation 13.8.* "*And all that dwell upon the earth shall worship him, whose names are not written in the book of life of* **the Lamb slain from the foundation of the world***."* The *"foundation of the world"* is equivalent to the expression *"from the beginning of creation" (Mark 10.6; 13.19).* Prior to creation, in the halls of heaven, the Lamb was considered slain.

God's salvation has always been a matter of faith and saves completely all who trust in Him. Although the physical sacrifice of Jesus' blood had not yet happened on earth its value in heaven was not lessened. Old Testament saints believed God and were justified with all rights and privileges of that justification. Their sins were covered - looking forward to the physical suffering of the Perfect Sacrifice and the shedding of the blood that was without spot, blemish, or taint of sin.

Do not be mistaken. No one can be saved apart from the shed blood of Jesus Christ, but the point is that, because of the blood, even the Old Testament saints were allowed audience with the King of kings. One day all who claim the blood of Christ will gather in glory – in the presence of God – to proclaim His greatness and goodness. Maybe we will sit down, eat a meal, and enjoy sweet communion with our friends and family – and our God and Savior. Won't it be wonderful there!

Goodness and Glory, Exodus 33.18

"And he said, I beseech thee, shew me thy glory." (Exodus 33.18)

Moses and several others saw God face-to-face, and ate a meal with Him. In our modern church terminology, that is called a "fellowship." What you will read in this article comes, in part, from speculation and somewhat from comparing Scripture with Scripture. Be assured that this author desires to exalt the name of our Lord above all else and it is with that intent we approach our subject.

Whenever I find a difficult passage in the Bible, there are three principles that I immediately apply. 1) I read to gain insight into the context. Much can be learned (and avoided) by knowing how the verse fits into the overall scheme of things. Someone rightly said that a text taken out of context is nothing more than a pretext. 2) I remember that God is infinitely intelligent and all-wise and I am tremendously limited due to a birth defect (the sin nature). If God were no smarter than I, He would not be God at all. There are some things that I simply will not understand and I will not, on this side of eternity, be able to discover. 3) I try to find in the Scripture application how that particular section exalts the Lord Jesus Christ since the entire Bible is "His-story" and points to Him.

With that in mind, I trust you will allow some latitude in my speculation – and accept this as a meditation attempting to give rest to my own questions and to exalt our Savior.

From reading the Scriptures, we know that there were some who had personal "sit-down at the table" conversations with God. *(Exodus 24.10, 11)* In this chapter the Bible says that *"the LORD spoke unto Moses face to face as a man speaketh unto his friend." (Exodus 33.11)* And, yes, the word *"face"* (**paniym** – *"an idiomatic expression that can refer to the entire person; also the face, one's mood, countenance, or attitude")* is the same Hebrew word in *Exodus 33.11 & 20.*

How is it that Moses could speak face to face with God in *verse 11* but was not allowed to see His face in *verse 20?* The closeness between Moses and God are revealed in the opportunity Moses had for the personal communion, but it also is seen in the fact that God said, *"I know thee by thy name." (Exodus 33.17)* Moses already realized that God knew his name because God had called him at the burning bush and several other times throughout the Exodus. God is here letting Moses know that this is a personal relationship between the two of them – something that not many attained prior to their death.

The answer to the first part of the question dealing with how Moses was allowed this special fellowship is based on the personal relationship between the two of them. A key to answering the second part, "Why could Moses not see God's face?" is revealed in Moses' question and God's answer. Many have noted when reading this selection that Moses asked to see God's glory (**kabod** – *"honor, glory, majesty, wealth"*) and God said He would make all His goodness (**tub** – *"property, goods, goodness, fairness, beauty"*) to pass before him. He further adds that He (God) would proclaim the name of the *"LORD"* (**Yahweh** – *the proper name for God in His covenant and saving relationship to man).*

It would make sense to call to our attention the understanding of God's goodness. He reveals Himself to us every day by His goodness, and has done so since the beginning of time. The goodness of God is a standard no matter the era, age, covenant, or dispensation in which someone lives.

The ultimate glory of God, however, is expressed in His desire, ability, and performance in the salvation of those who believe through Christ's shed blood. Nothing is more glorious than the fact that a holy God would save a lost sinner. (Please do not think this diminishes the brilliance and personal glory that coruscates from the presence of God's person.) The blood of Christ glorifies the Father each time someone believes. The perfect Lamb of God is the central figure in heaven and is the focus of every aspect of God's work on the earth and in heaven – from the Garden of Eden through the judgment of the Great Day of Christ. Everything in Scripture points to the Cross and the work accomplished there. It is all about Jesus Christ the Savior and His redemptive work.

The problem Moses faced was timing. Glory refers to the *"face, substance, and majesty"* of God. For Moses to see God's glory, He would see every part of the reality of Who God is and what He has done and shall do. Moses desired to see it all. But only *"when the fullness of the time was come, God sent forth his Son, made of a woman, made under the law." (Galatians 4.4)* So then what Moses requested was something not yet ready to be revealed but *"God having provided some better thing for us {those after the crucifixion of Christ}, that they without us should not be made perfect." (Hebrews 11.40)*

Daniel ran into a similar problem with timing in *Daniel 12*. He prophesied about the coming Tribulation Period, the Abomination of Desolations, and the resurrection of the dead; but he was stopped short by Michael, the archangel, with the command to *"seal up the book, even to the end of times." (Daniel 12.4)* It is very likely that Daniel was ready to reveal the account that is now contained in the New Testament book of the *Revelation*. Since the content of Daniel's prophetic chapters deal specifically with situations surrounding Christ's work of final redemption and the New Testament book of the *Revelation* is the *Revelation of Jesus Christ*, Daniel could go no further without revealing Christ Jesus Himself. The timing was wrong. Jesus had not died, shed His blood, or risen from the grave.

Moses faced the same dilemma. While under the Law, God would not, could not, reveal the Savior of mankind. The Old Testament sacrifices were impotent enough as they were *(Hebrews 10)*, but to reveal the personal work of the God-man would have rendered anything the priests did as second class.

God desires one's heart first and foremost. He had Moses' heart and Moses would lead the Israelites in their path toward God. If Moses had seen all there was to see of Jesus, his heart would never have been fully into the work of the Law. God showed His goodness when He passed by and maybe, on top of the mountain as Moses looked into the Promised Land, while he and God communed once more prior to Moses' death – maybe there God showed Moses His glory; and then Moses stepped out of this mortal into immortality to be alongside the God he loved.

Sinning in Ignorance, Leviticus 5.15-19

"If a soul commit a trespass, and sin through ignorance, in the holy things of the LORD; then he shall bring for his trespass unto the LORD a ram without blemish out of the flocks, with thy estimation by shekels of silver, after the shekel of the sanctuary, for a trespass offering." (Leviticus 5.15)

One of the great problems in modern society is the fact that most people have forgotten the concept of restitution. Some have become thieves, been caught, and released thinking that they could wait long enough to enjoy the "fruits" of their labors upon release from their incarceration. After the "time" is endured, they are then considered to have paid their debt to society. The problem is that time does not replace stolen money, missed opportunities, or lives that have been wasted or extinguished.

When coming to Christ, Zacchaeus understood fully this concept of restitution. *"And Zacchaeus stood, and said unto the Lord, Behold, Lord, the half of my goods I give to the poor; and* **if** *I have taken anything from any man by false accusation, I restore him four fold." (Luke 19.8)* Some have suggested that Zacchaeus was trying to purchase heaven through his generosity or to gain favor with the Master; but, that does not seem to be his intention. It seems more probable that he was convicted of his wrong and was trying to make things right.

In *Exodus 22* God gives the law of restitution. Restitution carries a variety of meanings dependent upon the context, but all are essentially linked to the idea of reciprocation and making amends. The Hebrew word is **shalam** and means *"to be safe"* or *"to be completed."* The word is normally used when God is keeping His people safe. In its simple form, this verb also means to be completed or to be finished – thus, leaving no loose ends to tie. Another meaning of this verb includes the idea of being at peace with another person (*Psalm 7.4*). **Shalam** also applies to the making of a treaty of peace (*Joshua 11.19; Job 5.23*); to pay or give a reward (*Psalm 62.12*); to restore, repay, or make retribution (*Exodus 21.36; Psalm 37.21*).

By application, restitution means to make peace by restoring things to their proper order. In the situation of the destruction of property or theft; the damaged or stolen item must be replaced. In the situation of a loss of ability to work due to injury, lost wages must be paid. Later, the Law added penalties for loss caused by deliberate actions. In the event that someone lost a limb or their life; the Law required an eye for an eye and a tooth for a tooth and a life for a life. Whatever was needed to restore, as nearly as possible, to its original state, and if restoration was impossible; judgment and penalty were prescribed. The major point is that restitution is required.

When Zacchaeus was pointed out by our Lord, he promised to repay anyone he had wronged. Since he used the word *"if"* it would seem that there were some he had defrauded of whom he was unaware. His attitude and actions were Scriptural according to *Leviticus 5.17,* *"... though he knew it not, yet he is guilty, and shall bear his iniquity."*

Whether the individual was aware of his sin or not did not change the fact of his guiltiness. Many people move about, living normal lives, completely unconvinced of their sin. Even many Christians speak of the universal sinfulness of mankind and the impossibility of attaining complete sanctification (i.e. sinless perfection) this side of heaven; but seldom, if ever, admit to their own personal sinfulness in specific terms. We are quick to admit that all have sinned and come short of the glory of God; but are slow to fall on our knees with a broken heart over our own desperate condition.

It does not matter if it is known sin or unknown sin – we shall stand guilty before God. The problem is not so much a difficulty with the known sin, but we may become overly concerned with our unknown sin. What should we do? Moses wrote of the remedy for unknown sin in *Leviticus* – a blood sacrifice. That was a sacrifice made often for sin that was known or unknown. Now, we have the perfect Sacrifice – the Lamb of God. His sacrifice is perfect and cleanses the believer from all sin – past, present, and future – both known and unknown. Jesus, with His shed blood, satisfied all the Law's demands for sacrifice.

The believer has been forgiven – completely! As a believer, we are able to rest in the finished work of our Great God and Savior Jesus Christ.

Familiarity Breeds Contempt, Numbers 1.53

"But the Levites shall pitch round about the tabernacle of testimony, that there be no wrath upon the congregation of the children of Israel: and the Levites shall keep the charge of the tabernacle of testimony." (Numbers 1.53)

As a pastor I have often been amused by the way people arrange themselves in their church seating. Quite often when I pray, I can pray for my congregation by thinking of the church setting and envisioning who is sitting where. By doing that, I am able to pray around the church for each member by name. Not very often someone will not sit in their "proper" place and it takes me a while to realize they are actually in church. A few weeks ago I greeted a man at the door of the church after Sunday morning service by telling him I had missed him the week before, but he was quick to let me know that he was actually there. After some consideration, and a bit of his irritation, we came to the conclusion that he had been sitting on the other side of the church.

Of course, in most churches, back rows come at a premium. Those pews are reserved for people who want to be at church but do not want to get the most from their religious experience. There are far too many distractions between themselves and the pulpit for them to be overly serious about the quiet stillness of meeting with God.

One particularly fine young lady that attends our church always sits on the front row when she comes alone, but on the back row when escorted by her boyfriend. She wants to get all she can with as few distractions as possible from the service while he seems content to simply be there with her.

Parents have a tremendous opportunity to protect their children (especially teenagers) from undue temptation by settling down with them or having them settle themselves down on the front row. I know that would be a fate worse than death itself, but I am certain you remember what it was like as a teenager in church yourself. There was much more boredom, yawning, passing notes, and other activities than we would like to recall. Just remember that your child is your child. What you did, he will do.

We have a responsibility to protect those placed under our care. *Leviticus 1.53* explains that the Levites were charged with a special duty – protection for Israel from God's wrath. Later on in the book (*Leviticus 3*), Moses delineates the specifics of caring for the Tabernacle which included setting it up, taking it down, transporting it, and general maintenance.

The Gershonites would care for all the coverings and adornments; the Kohathites would care for the furniture and fixtures; and the Merarites would care for the structure. But all those commands were secondary to their primary responsibility to protect Israel *"that there be no wrath upon the congregation."*

Too much familiarity with holy things often leads to a lax attitude. It seems that the preachers' and deacons' children often have a tougher time with the concept of God's holiness because they see the day-to-day work of the church and become familiar. That was the sin of Nadab and Abihu, Aaron's sons, who offered strange fire upon the altar of God. It was also the problem of Uzzah faced when he tried to steady the Ark of God when the Philistines returned it to Israel. As the oxen stumbled and the cart jostled, Uzzah reached to steady it. As he touched it, God struck him dead on the spot – too much familiarity with the sacred.

When people lose their respect for God; when they do not stand "amazed in the presence of Jesus the Nazarene;" they are in danger of God's wrath. When someone partakes of the Lord's Table unworthily (*"irreverently, in an unbecoming manner"*), they put themselves in a dangerous position. When church becomes just a place of "fellowship" and no longer a place to meet with a holy God, we must prepare ourselves for judgment.

The back row may be comfortable, but it usually is not the most sacred spot in the sanctuary. "Dressing down" may be convenient but it is probably not the best outfit for a meeting with the King of kings and Lord of lords.

One great line of defense for new believers and for young people is the protective example set by older (more mature) believers.

As did the Levites, we put a wall of protection between the wrath of God and those who would approach "unworthily." It is the responsibility of the New Testament believers (the New Testament priest) to guard carefully the sacredness of the holy things so that younger ones do not err out of ignorance.

Approach to God never indicated comfort first; but recognition of God's holiness. If in the Old Testament people approached God with reverence, should we not give to Him the same respect? Next Sunday, sit down front, pay close attention, take notes to review later, join in the worship, and stay awake. Let others know that you are excited to be in God's house, in His presence, and that you are fully alert to God's leading. By your example and through a loving attitude protect those young ones from being profane in the presence of God.

Shouting in the Church, Psalm 100.2

"Serve the LORD with gladness: come before his presence with singing." (Psalm 100.2)

Different churches exhibit vastly different styles of worship. I am often amused by the attitudes of those who take the opposite sides from each other on the issue of style.

I grew up in a small, rural Baptist church in North Carolina that was subdued in its worship. Once during a morning service a visitor hailed with a hearty "Amen!" and several of the regular attendees turned to see who had broken the sanctity of the moment. Several on the back row giggled because we had never heard anyone show such an animated display of enthusiasm. I believe a couple of sleepers actually opened their eyes for a moment.

Not long ago, I had the opportunity to jam (sing spontaneously) with some dear friends who were not Baptists. On the first evening of this particular conference, my three friends and I began singing some of the old songs during an intermission between services. There were four of us then, but it became a choir by the end of the week; and just the other day a lady who had joined us in singing called to tell me she was looking forward to next year. (None of the conference officials asked us to sing a special and even turned down our offer to do so. Maybe they are just not quite as enthusiastic in their spiritual life as we are.)

Although I suppose my personal preference for services is somewhere on the conservative side of the middle, there is something special about the spontaneous praise that comes from someone who is in love with his Lord and Savior.

Many churches have become so "dignified" that they expect the Holy Spirit to come in, sit down, and not stir things up – after all, what would the visitors think if someone began weeping over their sinfulness or the sinfulness of others. It would be quite difficult to explain how someone could be so full of the love of Christ that they should come to the altar and weep over God's goodness (at least not on Sunday morning – during "worship"). On Sunday mornings we should all ease in quietly, take our place, and begin our meditation so as to not disturb God's Spirit.

It is necessary to maintain order, but there should always be room for God's Spirit to work. I suppose that worked up emotions, in an attempt to give the appearance that the Spirit is involved, is just as distasteful as having no spirit at all. The Bible says *"For as many as are led by the Spirit of God, they are the sons of God." (Romans 8.14)*

The church service should be a time to which we give much consideration and prayer. Anytime there is no room for change, the Holy Spirit's work is hindered. That applies to loud, energetic services as well as quiet, subdued ones.

Every act of worship, however, should express what is in the heart. *Psalm 100.1* gives the standard for approach used by the Israelites as they presented themselves to God. They should *"make a joyful noise."* Many times we suggest that if people cannot carry a tune, they should at least make a joyful noise. The word from which *"make a joyful noise"* is translated is **rua**. It is a verb meaning to *"shout, or sound a blast."* The term occurs thirty-three times in the Old Testament and was used fundamentally to convey the action of shouting or of making a loud noise.

Prior to most services at our church, people gather around greeting each other and often are laughing. They are making a joyful noise unto the Lord. During the worship service each person should engage in enthusiastic singing. This singing refers to a cry of delight over a marvelous event – that of salvation and of being in God's presence. Paul exhorts believers to *"Speak to yourselves in psalms and hymns and spiritual songs, singing and making melody in your heart to the Lord." (Ephesians 5.19)* The singing, then, should be from a sated heart and spirit and not used to get people "fired up" for the service.

Psalm 100.2 gives two imperatives for approaching God. The second concerns singing and the first service. Part of our service toward God involves giving. Again, Paul exhorts believers to give cheerfully because the Lord loves a cheerful giver *(II Corinthians 9.7)*. Although the Greek word (**hilaros**) resembles the English word *"hilarious"* it does not carry the same connotation. The word denotes a happy, glad, or cheerful state of mind and not one overcome with laughter or mirth. It does not indicate someone affected by humor.

The point is that whether you are animated or subdued in your worship, it should be a matter of the heart. When you sing, it should not be for show but from a heart of praise. When you give, it should not be for others to see but from a heart of praise. When you attend church, it should not be for what you receive but from a heart of praise.

As we enter into our fellowship of praise with God, we should already have a heart filled with praise and singing before the first announcement is made or the first note of a song is played. We should come before His presence with singing – not hoping that something will bless us. The blessing should already be in our hearts and on our lips.

The Fullness of Time, Galatians 4.4, 5

"But when the fulness of the time was come, God sent forth his Son, made of a woman, made under the law, To redeem them that were under the law, that we might receive the adoption of sons." (Galatians 4.4, 5)

We all know exactly what these verses mean and have been convinced through preaching and careful study of their various applications. In God's mind, somewhere in eternity past, He determined a plan to create and to redeem after that creation had failed (*Acts 2.23; Revelation 13.8*). The fact that God, with His perfect knowledge, would create a people, knowing they would almost immediately rebel, is staggering to say the least; but, it all points to the loving God who desires to love and bless His creation.

During the decision process by God, He also selected the perfect time in human history for the Messiah to step onto the scene and the perfect method of His delivery. It was not the political pressure of taxation that drove Joseph and Mary to Bethlehem but God who had determined this beforehand (*Micah 5.2*). It was not the threat of death by an insane tyrant that drove the family from their home to Egypt (*Hosea 11.1*), but God who predetermined it.

These verses tell us that the time was right for the coming of the Messiah. It was all a part of God's plan that Jesus would be born of a virgin and born under the law (*Isaiah 7.14*). All things were in place. The universal language was *koine* Greek – the common language of the people. The Romans had built roads that made travel from one place to another more convenient. Because of the diversity of gods, many were ready for a God who was a true God and not the extension of someone's fanciful emotions (*Acts 17.23*).

All was ready. Into this cultured, cosmopolitan, and civilized world the Messiah came. Some of the greatest things He did were not things He did at all. It only seems right that when God took upon Himself the form of a man he would begin to institute some radical changes in society. It should be obvious that slavery and crucifixion were never intended to be a part of God's plan for humanity. It is unthinkable that a kind, gentle Jesus would not rush in and destroy the wicked institutions that were fomenting those dastardly deeds upon their fellow man. In fact, the only institutions He spoke out against involved organized religion – not government.

Today the church is organized and operating. Just the other day I read of a church that had a beauty salon, barber shop, aerobics, sauna, fitness center, and many other extras for their worshipers. Others are involved in correcting all of the social and political ills that are rife within our nation.

Even though many good ideas are espoused, often good is not the best. When Jesus was on the earth, His faithful entourage numbered twelve (with a few others that supported financially or came and went). When the masses followed He thinned them out by suggesting they would live a life of hardship and suffering. Although He had the power (and certainly the resources), Jesus never built a gymnasium, social club, or dance hall; neither did He participate in a "sit-in," political demonstration, a massive write-in campaign, or protest.

Jesus was acutely aware of religious hypocrisy and political intolerance, yet, not once did He cry out asking for solidarity against an ungodly government (*Mark 12.17*). Rather than taking a stand against the government, Jesus seemed to support it. Under the inspiration of the Holy Spirit Paul wrote that we should obey the government so long as government does not overstep our opportunity to follow God's law (*Romans 13.1*). Could it be possible that the Roman government was ordained by God? Yes! All governments are, as well as their leaders, set up and taken down by God Himself. All kings and those in authority are under the supervision of God and can do nothing apart from His pleasure (*Proverbs 21.1*). It matters not whether the king is godly or ungodly – God is still in control. Just as truly as the Babylonian government during Daniel's time was ordained by God, so is every government.

Daniel outlasted several kings and at least four kingdoms and the only time we hear a word of protest is from a submissive heart to his superior when asking leave not to eat of unclean food (*Daniel 1.8-16*). Daniel protested neither against the fiery furnace nor against the image Nebuchadnezzar had set up.

His silence during Belshazzar's drunken party shows that he was not out front picketing against the king's foul character, the orgy on the inside, or his political policy concerning civil rights and religious freedoms. None of that violated his personal purity before God and Daniel trusted God to do His work in His way. The only time Daniel speaks is after he is brought in by Belshazzar and specifically asked for an interpretation of the handwriting on the wall (*Daniel 5.13*).

So what is the point? Is it wrong to have a gymnasium or to be active in politics? Not at all. That misses the point as badly as thinking the world can be changed by legislation or by lively church services. The point is that Jesus did not come into the world to reform the world – He came into the world to redeem it. He did not come to make governments fair but to save the lost.

Jesus was born at the right time according to God's perfect timing. It was a time of political unrest, spiritual disillusionment, and societal subjugation. Into this world came our Savior and sought to redeem souls – one by one – from the eternal results of sin. As followers of Christ, our main ministry should be seeking souls not changing governments. It should be reaching the lost not toning the body.

The Church is a kingdom within a nation. Our citizenship is not of this world – we are all aliens by birth. As aliens we do not rise up against the foreign power under which we live, but we aggressively seek to grow our Father's kingdom by inviting others to be a part of it. According to our Founder's example (*Hebrews 12.1, 2*), we are not involved in reformation, but in transformation (*Romans 12.2*).

Taken for Granted, Philemon 1.21

"Having confidence in thy obedience I wrote unto thee, knowing that thou wilt also do more than I say." (Philemon 1.21)

The book of Philemon is obviously about three people: a slave owner, a slave, and an arbiter. The slave is Onesimus who had evidently not been a good slave (*Philemon 1.11*) and probably had run away from his master. While on the run he met Paul, the apostle, who showed him the way of salvation. Onesimus believed and was saved.

Philemon, the one after which the book is named, was a slave owner who also happened to be a believer. He evidently was a godly man because Paul refers to him in very flattering terms. We should remember that this book is not specifically addressing the problem of slavery – whether it is right or wrong (that conclusion seems obvious), politically correct or politically incorrect. It addresses something far greater than governmental regulations or acceptable legal practices.

Paul is the arbiter. Having known Philemon through the ministry and labor in the cause of Christ, Paul knew he could depend on Philemon to do the right thing. Because they were brothers in Christ, they had a common bond that now included the runaway slave, Onesimus.

That introduces the characters but it should be apparent that the major player in the text is not Onesimus. Only a small portion of the whole is dedicated to him and his condition. Paul argues several goods point on Onesimus' behalf which all relate in some fashion to their new relationship within God's family. These are all points that, sooner or later, Philemon would understand on his own.

Paul mentions the fact that Onesimus is now a believer and requests that he be treated as such. He further reports on Onesimus' profitability to Paul in the ministry and asks Philemon to consider the same assets. Finally, on the plus side, Paul explains how he would like for Onesimus to stay with him but did not want to assume too much (*Philemon 1.14*).

The remainder of the epistle concerns Paul and Philemon and their relationship to each other. Paul reminisces about their past ministry together in church and out of church. He remembers fondly their common friends and co-workers. Paul mentions further of Philemon's testimony of love and good works. He then calls upon his friend for help.

I have held for sometime the philosophy that when someone takes you for granted it is not necessarily a bad thing. Being taken for granted shows that you are trusted because past events have shown your reliability. For example, when approaching a door, my wife will stop and wait for me to open it for her. She takes it for granted that I will do just that. Once we were shopping in a small town in our two-door car. After every stop, I had moved around to open my wife's door and help her out. Our backseat rider soon was frustrated with the delays and asked my wife if the door was broken. We now have been married for over thirty-one years and my wife still takes me for granted – and I enjoy it.

In Paul's plea there are places where he takes Philemon for granted. One concerns their relationship. Paul has been away as a prisoner but he takes no second thought that Philemon feels any differently toward him. In other words, Paul takes it for granted that Philemon is growing in grace and not going backwards. The normal Christian life is that of progression. Those who go backwards in faith or drop out all together do not bring glory to our great God.

He takes for granted that Philemon will receive Onesimus as warmly as Paul sends him. It does not matter what is his rank in society, past wrongs, or debts; Paul knows how Philemon will respond. Paul's assumption of Philemon's Christian grace was accurate but not wanting to rob Philemon of his blessing of giving, Paul sent Onesimus back (*Philemon 1.14*).

Even though Paul makes a request for Philemon to forgive Onesimus' debt, he has no doubt it will happen because Paul has no means of paying. Paul commends Onesimus as a servant of Christ and a brother.

One last thing Paul takes for granted is Philemon's Christian hospitality. He says, "*. . . prepare me also a lodging. . . .*" *(Philemon 1.22)* He assumes that Philemon will make room for him.

How would you feel if someone took you for granted? Even when they assume that you are growing in the Lord it would be nice to be asked rather than assumed. Hospitality, it seems, should not be take for granted. Paul did not ask for a bed. He told Philemon to have one ready. Most of us would think, "How dare him!"

The feeling of being taken for granted is based on a wrong attitude. When you are dating or first married it is a joy to hold the door open for her or to wait for him to open it. As the relationship moves on the joy turns into inconvenience. "Why can't she open the door for herself?" Although that is very simplistic, it does illustrate the fact that while the relationship is vibrant nothing seems to be mundane or inconvenient – nothing gives the sense of being taken for granted. All is fresh and alive. All brings joy. All is good so long as the relationship is good.

Paul and Philemon, separated by many miles and prison bars; had a wonderful, vibrant relationship. As you enter your church this week, remember that this is a place of relationships. The fact that no one fusses over you should let you know that you are expected – they take your faithfulness for granted. When you are imposed upon to do some task, thank God that they take your servant's spirit for granted.

On the other hand, if, when you walk into your church people do make a fuss over you, maybe you have lacked the faithfulness it takes to be taken for granted.

To Be as Gods, Genesis 3.5

"For God doth know that in the day ye eat thereof, then your eyes shall be opened, and ye shall be as gods, knowing good and evil." (Genesis 3.5)

What makes sin so compelling and alluring is the promise of something we do not have that we think we want. All temptation promises to give us some special freedom, gift, attention, sensation, or other enhancement to our lives that is attractive. After all, temptation would be easily resisted if the thing offered was not so, well – tempting.

Another aspect of any temptation is the element of truth that is involved. Every temptation offers some of the truth but certainly not all of it. Drinking alcoholic beverages does make one feel better – for a time. Taking illegal drugs does give one a "high." None of that would be appealing if some truth was not involved. Of course the problem is exacerbated by the selected, alluring information offered to the one being tempted.

If the alcoholic or drug addict knew completely their end, they most probably would have reconsidered the first act of imbibing. Had Adam and Eve known the ultimate result of their decision concerning the fruit, I am certain their decision would have been different.

In the temptation of Adam and Eve, what was so alluring was the offer of some truth of which they were completely unaware. There was nothing else they could possibly have desired. The vehicle for the temptation and sin was the fruit, but the real draw was the offer of a truth that was hidden from them. They would be like a god because they would know the secret that only God (and the Serpent) knew.

At this point in time, prior to the first sin, the couple was innocent but not righteous. A person cannot claim to be right unless he had made a decision – a right decision. What Adam and Eve did not realize was that had they made the right decision, they would have known good and evil by virtue of their right choice. They would have had the knowledge without the sin, guilt, and consequences involved.

The serpent did not tell them that. He only told them what he wanted them to know in order to accomplish his objective. The person who never takes a drink or never uses illegal drugs simply needs to see wrecked lives in order to know where those substances lead. In essence, choosing to abstain gives one the freedom with the knowledge but without all the problems.

We must consider another thought that may be valid in understanding the entire scenario. God is always ultimately in control. It is His will for us to grow (and was for the first couple) in knowledge and experience. Most of that knowledge comes from experimental learning (i.e. hands-on experimentation). Since Satan was God's anointed cherub, it would follow that he would be privy to much of God's plan. He, very possibly, knew that God created within mankind an insatiable desire for knowledge. He drew upon that longing and thereby set the trap for the Fall.

It is possible that Satan knew, in eternity, mankind was designed to learn and grow. One day, apart from sin, Adam and Eve would have all their desires satisfied, but they took a short-cut. The offer of knowledge was always in God's plan, but the corruption came in the timing.

In this life, because of sin, we learn slowly and with many misconceptions. Our knowledge is smeared with the reality of sin and wrongly aimed desires. Now we struggle and strive for that which would have come to our parents (Adam and Eve) naturally.

When God redeems His creation in the ultimate redemption, He will provide for us the "knowledge of good and evil." Then we will be able to learn and know all those things but without the possibility for sinning. The partial truth Satan offered, God will one day offer in perfection and completion. What Satan could offer only as man disobeyed, God will offer without complication.

One day, in eternity, God will answer all questions and He will allow us unlimited opportunity for complete satisfaction of all our curiosities. Not only will there be no sin or guilt attached to our actions, but in our eternal bodies, there will be no possibility for sinning.

Now we struggle with right and wrong – good and bad – and the consequences of our decisions. Then, in His presence, struggles will be over and we will enjoy the New Creation and our Creator forever.

The Powers that Be, Romans 13.1, 2

"Let every soul be subject unto the higher powers. For there is no power but of God: the powers that be are ordained of God. Whosoever therefore resisteth the power, resisteth the ordinance of God: and they that resist shall receive to themselves damnation." (Romans 13.1, 2)

It would seem that the church has fallen into some troublous times in recent years. Many in religious leadership have called for a united front against the ever encroaching political machine that is robbing us of our religious freedoms. We are urged to get involved, to stand up for our rights, and to rescue America from the oppression of Satan.

Each Christian should be concerned about the direction our nation is taking and for the spiritual problems within it; however, one would be remiss to find in Scripture any Christian who tried to meld Christianity with government or the political system of its times.

As a Roman citizen, Paul probably had more clout than any other early Christian mentioned in the Bible. He was a ranking official who, through his influence, could have made a difference in the government. He could have drawn upon his influence and friends to stage protests, marches, and sit-ins – or possibly even amass enough support to march on Rome itself. It seems that Paul had a much different attitude than the modern Christian or church member of today.

To say that the times were different then is not a good argument. Although records cannot be found to point specifically to the practice of abortions and the existence of abortion clinics, evidence has been presented from historical records showing that ancient Egypt was involved in this practice. Knowing of the medical practices and advancements in medical technology, experimentations, and understanding; it would not be stretching facts to assume there were abortions for convenience sake during Rome's zenith. Paul never speaks of or alludes to this most detestable form of murder.

We know from common knowledge that slavery was a norm for the day. During this time some of the most brutal and grotesque forms of entertainment ever to be conceived by the depraved mind of man existed – and thrived; yet against these things Paul was silent. One of the most stunning thoughts in all of this is that our Lord was silent in regard to governmental abuse and the murder of citizens. When asked about the heavy taxation, our Lord replied, *"Render therefore unto Caesar the things which are Caesar's and unto God the things that are God's." (Matthew 22.21)*

How could Paul and our Lord take such a pacifistic position when thousands were being abused daily? How could they not petition the government, run for office, protest, or in some other way get involved? As you study the Scriptures, you will notice that the New Testament saints did not even lead rescue missions to seek the release of their leaders – they were normally somewhere, in seclusion - praying (of all things!). This is so contrary to our modern concept of the church and state it seems as though it must have come from another religion – certainly not Christianity.

The difference between early New Testament believers and today's modern Christians is one of citizenship. While we Christians have a wonderful, God-given and blessed land; we cannot lay a stronger claim to it than to our eternal home. It may have been easier for the early Christians to not lay claim to Rome as their home country because it was neither Israel nor a godly state. The persecutions would also create a natural division between those believers and the state. For those of us who are in the United States of America, living in a nation founded on God's Word, we often lose sight of the fact that this world (including our beloved nation) is not our home.

Since we are citizens of another country, we are living here on temporary visas. The early Christians knew that and lived their lives according to that principle. In *Romans 13.1 & 2*, Paul explains in detail our personal responsibility to civil government and before God. Paul's principle concerning a civil (or any other) chain of command is that we are responsible to be subject (**hupotasso** – *"to place in an orderly fashion"*) unto the higher powers. In other words, while I am ultimately responsible to God, as the head of my household, I am immediately responsible to my government and its laws.

It seems a bit extreme to think that the power of Rome, in all its vileness, was ordained by God – but it was. As a matter of fact, Daniel spoke of Rome when he interpreted Nebuchadnezzar's dream in *Daniel 2*. Although situations may not seem overly spiritual, God is still in control. Kings and tyrants may believe they are in power but *"there is no power but of God: the powers that be are ordained of God." (Romans 13.16)*

The application is obvious, but Paul continues by explaining that *"Whosoever . . . resisteth the power, resisteth the ordinance of God: . . ." (Romans 13.2a)* According to Paul's words (which are inspired by God), when a Christian resists the government, whether in speeding violations or tax evasion, it is a sin against God's holy ordinance. In the final phrase of verse two Paul expresses the fact that those who resist the powers that be will find themselves in judgment (**krima** {*destruction*} – *"the results of judgment"*).

So then, we must ask the questions, "Is it ever right to disobey the law?" The answer is "Yes, if the law is in variance with God's Word." The Bible says we are to obey the higher powers. So long as the law does not attempt to force the Christian in to sin, he is obligated to obey it. In so doing, I am being obedient to God.

Three Tabernacles, Luke 9.33

"And it came to pass, as they departed from him, Peter said unto Jesus, Master, it is good for us to be here: and let us make three tabernacles; one for thee, and one for Moses, and one for Elias: not knowing what he said." (Luke 9.33)

The twelve had just returned from a miracle-working campaign (*Luke 9.1-6*) and had witnessed Jesus' tremendous power for physical provision by feeding well over 5,000 people (there were 5,000 men, *Luke 9.14*). After these exceptional displays of power over physical problems, Jesus asked His disciples for their take on the results of these miracles.

"Who say the people that I am?" Most of the people were claiming that Jesus was either a resurrected John the Baptist, Elijah, or one of the other Old Testament prophets (*Luke 9.19*). One of the great Old Testament prophets, along with Elijah, was Moses. These two men were the greatest of all time in the minds of nearly every Israelite. To suggest that the people thought of Jesus as either Moses or Elijah would indicate their great respect and admiration for Him.

Having a consensus of the local people did not make this personal for the disciples. As was the usual goal for our Savior, He brought people to a place of making personal decisions and personal stands for their beliefs. He never left someone in the same condition as He found them. After performing and being a part of a vibrant, but mostly physical ministry, Jesus wanted them to understand the difference between physical and spiritual blessings.

"But who say ye that I am?" Peter responded with, *"Thou art the Christ, the Son of the Living God."* To go from that to the transfiguration experience with Peter's attempt at making Christ equal with Moses and Elijah seems a bit far-reaching. The narrative tells us that Peter, James, and John had been sleeping (*Luke 9.32*) and were most probably a little (if not totally) groggy. Laying aside the fact that they were asleep (as seemed to be the case often when Jesus was involved in deep spiritual battles) or so tired they were unable to think spiritual thoughts does not free them from the responsibility of growing from their

experiences. They had healed the sick, fed the multitudes, and raised the dead.

What could they have been thinking? Was this a matter of not separating between physical and non-physical (material and spiritual)? Can anything short of the Word of God actually make that distinction? (*Hebrews 4.12*) When we are faced with this question, we must understand that the physical is bonded with the spiritual so that we cannot separate between the two.

Peter must have been trying to make this type of distinction because he had seen the tremendous physical power that could only have resulted from spiritual power. It would also seem obvious that in His exhortation eight days prior to the transfiguration (*Luke 9.22-27*), Jesus made a strong point of the need to set aside physical affections so that the path to discipleship may be clear.

Many have suggested that Peter was trying to put Jesus on a similar plane with Moses and Elijah - that he was raising Jesus to the highest possible position within the ranks of Israel's venerable saints. In this view, the ones holding it suggest that Moses and Elijah disappeared to show Jesus stands uniquely apart from all others. Admittedly, this is the most widely held position and possibly could be the correct one.

Remembering that the theme of these writings is *"Uncommon Views of Common Verses,"* I would offer somewhat of a different perspective. Since Peter had already confessed Jesus to be distinctly *"The Christ of God,"* to suggest that he now was struggling with Christ's identity would send him backward in his walk of faith. The answer seems to rest upon the distinction already made (between Christ and the other prophets) and the distinction that needed to be made (between the material and spiritual) in the minds of other followers.

The masses followed Jesus largely because of His ability to provide for them physically. Jesus did not come to feed but to save – He did not come to heal but to redeem. The fact that He did heal and feed only muddied the waters further in Peter's mind. It is quite possible that Peter wanted the three tabernacles in order to make a distinction between the three personalities. After all, he did not suggest that they share one tabernacle. In doing this, there would have been a clear line of demarcation between Moses, Elijah, and the Christ of God.

As soon as Peter made the suggestion, Moses and Elijah vanished with God's blessing falling specifically on Jesus (*Luke 9.35, 36*). The point is that Jesus does not take second place and, in first place, He shares that honor with no one. It is also obvious that God rejected the idea of a physical building in which to house His Son. The honor of being Savior would be shared with no one and no thing. He stands distinctly alone. Further, their silence (*Luke 9.36*) suggests to us that the Holy Spirit, not man, is the One who enlightens men's minds.

Building a tabernacle with great embellishments will not bring glory to God – often those "adornments" in houses of worship actual detract from one's ability to worship God in *Spirit and in Truth*. Whoever comes to Christ must do so by the invitation of the Spirit – not by man's wisdom or devices. Peter was attempting, in his own power, to do the work of the Holy Spirit. His attitude was noble, but, like many eager saints today, he was attempting to do the work that only God can do.

Rather than building more tabernacles, maybe we should be awake and alert during prayer time. Maybe we should be keenly aware of the work God is doing and allow Him to have His full glory in doing it.

What Happened to the Sabbath? Matthew 12.8; Mark 2.27

"For the Son of man is Lord even of the sabbath day." (Matthew 12.8)

As a part of the original Creation, God established the pattern for man's work week. He set up the week as being seven days – the last of which would be a day of rest and rejoicing in the finished Creative work of God (*Genesis 2.2, 3*).

The Sabbath was further authorized as a day of rest by a direct fiat from God as one of the Ten Commandments (*Exodus 20.9-11*). One "bone of contention" to which the Pharisees often referred when dealing with our Lord concerned His lack of keeping the Sabbath. The fact is that the Pharisees incorporated so many restrictions for keeping the Sabbath; no one was able to completely comply.

On one specific occasion, while Jesus and His disciples were walking through the grain field (which in itself was a violation of Sabbath laws) being hungry, they picked some of the grain, rubbed it in their hands to remove the husk, and ate it. The Pharisees, who must have been lurking – waiting for an opportunity against Jesus, were quick to point out their sin.

In response to their antagonistic attacks, Jesus set forth a new understanding of the Sabbath's purpose. *"The Sabbath was made for man, and not man for the Sabbath: Therefore the Son of man is Lord also of the Sabbath." (Mark 2.27, 28)*

The Pharisees were of the conviction (and rightly so from the Mosaic Law) that man and his movements were drastically restricted by the Sabbath observances. The Sabbath; originally intended to be a day of rest, relaxation, and worship; had devolved into a day of legalism and suspicions.

When Jesus asserted the fact that He was the Lord of the Sabbath, He was stating His deity and authority over all creation. Further, He was setting forth a prophecy of the coming change in objects of sacred worship.

From the beginning of time, mankind was pointed to the completed Creation as his focal point of satisfaction. It was the end of the work week for which he longed – the ending of the week - when labor was complete. Other than a future Sabbath rest promised for believers in Christ, the Sabbath stands alone as the only one of the Ten Commandments that is not specifically reiterated in the New Testament.

The moral and ethical rules for living and biblical philosophy for relationships do not change; however, the day we call the Sabbath has been replaced by something better. The *"better"* is Christ. Described as *better things*, the attributes and work of our crucified Savior describe His work in fulfilling what the Law and the Prophets required concerning the Sabbath. Prior to the incarnation; (Jesus' receiving of a physical body through the birth process, *John 1.14*) all that the world had to look forward to was the possibility of rest at the end of a long work day. The Sabbath was the celebration of that rest held each Saturday.

For New Testament believers, the day has changed as well as the reason for observing a special day. The death of our Lord, in essence, also put to death the need for the Sabbath and also instituted a focus for our worship. On the first day of the week, early in the morning, the worshippers found the stone rolled away and the Savior gone (*Matthew 28.1-6*).

Because of the resurrection, we do not celebrate the end of Creation, but rather the new Creation brought about as a result of the saving power of a living Lord. We are not merely to sit and rest – waiting for something to happen. It has already happened and we are to tell those who do not know quickly (*Matthew 28.7*).

While Old Testament believers had nothing to do in his celebration, we have much to do – we have a risen Savior to proclaim. If in the Old Testament Sabbatical culture, people were to abstain from secular, unnecessary activity; how much more should we, who are the children of light, do only those things that honor our Lord on the weekly day of celebration for His resurrection?

It seems that the Christian has fallen into the worldly philosophy (and possibly the worldly religion) that suggests Saturday and Sunday are the *"weekend."* Please remember that Saturday (the Old

Testament Sabbath) is the weekend and Sunday (the New Testament day of resurrection) is the week-beginning. Let us maintain the sacredness of our celebration by giving that day fully and completely to our Savior. Sunday should be a day of activity – not secular, but sacred – not of mowing the lawn, but of singing in the choir – not or fishing and camping, but of fellowship and Christian community.

We should carefully guard the Lord's Day so that our light may lighten the dark hearts around us with the splendor of our risen Savior. Is it sinful to do secular work on Sunday? That question misses the point. All activity should point people to the Savior and encourage them to worship the One True God. Does mowing your grass on Sunday, for example, let your unsaved neighbor know that you serve a risen Savior that you honor on His special day?

The Positive Side of Separation, II Corinthians 6.17

"Wherefore come out from among them, and be ye separate, saith the Lord, and touch not the unclean *thing;* and I will receive you." (II Corinthians 6.17)

Although we know our Lord was tempted in every area of His life as we who believe are, it just seems there are more "things" out there that draw our attention than there possibly could have been during that time. As a young boy the "things" that could be used to gain my attention seemed, by today's standards, mundane enough that today's young people would rather laugh at them than join in those out-dated activities.

Things that were strictly forbidden forty years ago are now accepted practices. Many of the arguments for condescending are true. For example, going to movie theaters was strictly forbidden in our home and church. Only the "city" church people attended – after all, the theater was the place Hollywood spewed out its venom.

The argument today that "we don't have anything to do" does not seem to hold water because there is much more to do now than there was in the 1960s in rural North Carolina just outside of Carthage (you have probably never heard of that county seat before – population 1,900). The argument that works sounds something like this: "It's no different from renting a movie and taking it home or watching it on cable." That holds water until we ask ourselves, "Why are we so set on watching that stuff anyway?"

A great problem in our churches is that we have not come out but rather have dived in. We are no longer set apart but have become part of the group. If we hold to the view that the movies, playing cards, and moderate social drinking are acceptable practices then we truly have become one of the worldly crowd and have relegated all of the old-time revivalist preachers to the scrapheap of irrelevance.

There are traits that seem trivial when considered against the grand scheme of things such as building a church and drawing in crowds; but Paul, while under the authority and inspiration of God's

Spirit wrote, *"Come out from among them and be ye separate . . . and touch not the unclean thing."* If we relegate the old-time preachers to a place of irrelevancy, we must do the same to the Apostle Paul and Christ Himself.

To preach separation for the sake of being separate, however, is to dwell too long on the negative "don'ts" in Scripture without speaking of the positives. There are many positive reasons the Bible speaks of being separate. Separation from the world (*come out*) is more of a normal action taken when the Christian is absorbed by the love of Christ. The areas of separation to the believer who loves his Savior more than life itself finds that things of the world have no appeal because they pale in the shadows created by the effulgent glory of the risen Christ.

The fact that we are to be separate from the world finds its foundation in the fact that God has already separated His children from others. *"But know that the Lord hath set apart him that is godly for himself: the Lord will hear when I call unto him."* (Psalm 4.3) This choosing was done prior to man's creation. It is an amazing thought when we understand that God had known all along who would be His and He planned for us to do His will. It is all *"According as he hath chosen us in him before the foundation of the world, that we should be holy and without blame before him in love."* (Ephesians 1.4)

For someone to claim a relationship with God without being separated to God and from the world is, at best, a crime against God's holiness and a smack against His integrity. He said, *"Be ye holy, for I am holy."* The above two verses state clearly that the true believer has been predestined to live a life of holiness (separation) to God (see *Ephesians 1*).

All of the aforementioned thoughts simply remind the believer of some negatives the world sees as they look in (and some believers) who see only the restrictions associated with a sanctified life. Peter writes, however, to help dispel such negative ideas with some poignant and succinct concepts mentioned only in nutshells that should excite even a less than enthusiastic follower of Christ. Peter writes, *"But ye are a chosen generation, a royal priesthood, a holy nation, a peculiar people; that ye should show forth the praises of him who hath called you out of darkness into his marvelous light."* (I Peter 2.9)

The fact is that we are not simply called out of the world but specifically to God. We are a specially selected offspring (*"chosen generation"* – see *Ephesians 1.4-6; Psalm 4.3*). Do you remember in the playground days when captains were selected to choose teams? Being the first chosen was always exciting but there was a certain stigma connected with being chosen last. All the forethought and deliberation was used in choosing the first and the best players. Peter says that those selected by God were chosen through a thoughtful and deliberate process. When the time came for choosing His family, you were first on His mind.

The believer is also separated into a class of royal priests. These royal priests stood in distinct separation from all the rest of Israel and in distinction from the priests in general. Royal priests were those who were worthy of making sacrifices to the king – especially to the King of kings. Israel, in contrast to the world, was such a *"chosen generation (nation)"* of set apart (separated unto God as holy) group of royal priests. Baal worshippers had their priests yet none of those priests could so much as approach the King's throne. The priesthood of New Testament believers are called to a royal dominion and clothed with royal dignity (*Revelation 1.6; 20.6*), which separates them from the world and makes them fit for royal service. The world of the lost has no such opportunity.

Peter also refers to the believers as a holy nation. Again, holy means to be set apart and nations speak of a distinct ethnic group. Since, in Christ, the walls of distinction between male, female, nationality, and ethnicity have been erased (*Galatians 2.28*); the believers are separated into a new group – the Church of the Living God. Because of the erasure of physical distinctions and the imbuement of the Holy Spirit, believers have a special relationship of which the world has no understanding. We are, in essence, separated from the world and into a most remarkable relationship with each other – the body of Christ and the family of God.

Peter mentions that the believer is a peculiar person. The same concept is utilized in *Exodus 19.5, 6* when God chose out Israel to be His special people. They would be (and still are) a peculiar people. Peculiar does not mean strange, odd, or eccentric. It means a special possession. God calls them His jewels (*Malachi 3.17*). Jewels! Imagine that!

From an out-of-fellowship sort of vantage point, being separated seems to indicate a position akin to punishment or disciplinary actions; however, from God's perspective it is a place of honor. Over thirty years ago my wife and I separated ourselves from all others and became one together in marriage. Separation from all others ushered us into a lifetime of blessing many people never experience. Neither of us feels burdened down by restrictions because of the relationship we have – we desire no other. God has truly blessed us by delivering us from the world system and into each others' arms (*Luke 1.74, 75*). So it is, too, with the believers' separation to God. We are freed to serve Him completely.

One final aspect of separation that must draw our attention is that of the end of time. The Bible teaches that the saved will be separated at the Coming of Christ, in the judgments, and in eternity. Looking back over all of this may prove that separation is not such a bad thing after all. Being separated to God on earth for the short while we are here seems to be a small and trivial sacrifice when viewed alongside eternity in a home specifically prepared for us (*II Corinthians 4.17; John 14.1-3*).

It was Jim Eliot who said, "He is no fool who gives up that which he cannot keep to gain that which he cannot lose."

What was the Real Problem? Matthew 25.1-12

"When shall these things be? and what shall be the sign of thy coming, and of the end of the world?" (Matthew 24.3)

We must carefully describe the setting for this parable or else it could lead into terrible error (if not outright heresy). In *Matthew 24* Jesus gives what is commonly called the "Olivet Discourse" in answering His disciples' questions, *"When shall these things be? and what shall be the sign of thy coming, and of the end of the world?" (Matthew 24.3)*

Following their question, Jesus gives, in brief, the future of the Jewish nation from the time of the destruction of the Temple (*Matthew 24.2*) until the Glorious Appearing of Christ at His second coming to the earth (*Matthew 25.29, 30*). It is vital to understand that *Matthew 24* is addressed specifically to the Jewish people concerning their nation. Thus, the narrative takes the listener from their present time through history, into the Great Tribulation period, and into the Kingdom (Millennial reign of Christ).

It is with that earthly, one thousand year reign in mind that Jesus offers His parable of the ten virgins. Of these ten virgins, five are considered wise and five are foolish. Some have attempted to place this event at the time of the Rapture only to find the parallels failing miserably. In order to understand this parable, we must understand the setting and significance of the various parts of the story – remember that all ten are virgins. That means none have defiled themselves by worshipping the god of this world. That particular application has never been addressed with Gentiles in mind, but only concerning the Jews who do not follow the Antichrist of the Tribulation period (*Revelation 14.4*).

Notice, too, that all ten were together in their walk to see the Bridegroom. It would seem they were each, at least by association, related to each other in agreement concerning the Bridegroom's coming. Even today, during the Seder, the Jewish people look for the coming of the prophet Elijah who is to herald the Messiah's advent. Their waiting is a part of the longing within the Jewish heart today and will only intensify after the Church is removed and the time of Jacob's

Trouble begins. These all waited – watched – and longed for deliverance at the hand of their Messiah.

It is also true that each of the ten virgins had lamps and each had some oil. The wise carried an extra container while the foolish carried only what the lamp would hold. The standard interpretation considers the foolish to be in need of oil – representing the Holy Spirit. The problem for many is in the effort to explain how some could have the Holy Spirit and then consider Him to be "used up." Is it possible for someone to use all the Holy Spirit and in the end find they have none available? This interpretation neither works with the thought of losing one's salvation nor with sinning away ones day of grace. There are places in Scripture that suggest the Holy Spirit's influence may be removed, but nowhere is there the slightest indication that He may be consumed into oblivion.

It is here that we must return to the setting and understand the environment. During the Great Tribulation, loyalty to the Antichrist will be tested by one's submission to a forced application of a mark (called the mark of the beast, *Revelation 13.17, 18*). Once someone takes the Beast's mark, he will have sold his opportunity for salvation, the Holy Spirit will no longer be a factor in drawing him to salvation, and he will have become an adulterer (impure – no longer a virgin, *Revelation 14.9; 17.2, 5; 18.3, etc.*).

Up to the point of taking the beast's mark, all have opportunity to believe and be sealed by the Father (*Revelation 7.2, 3; 9.4; 14.1; 22.4*) because God promised to pour out His Spirit upon all flesh (and especially the Jews) during this period of time (*Joel 2.28, 29*). As it is today, so it shall be during the Great Tribulation – the spirit that allows prophecy is not necessarily the Spirit that saves (*Matthew 7.22*) or the one who gives power for good works. Many people have, and will have, enough enlightenment by the Holy Spirit to be able to know they have a need to meet the Bridegroom because the end of the world is near; but they will not have had a salvation, regenerating, experience that provides resurrection from a spiritually dead state. It is the Holy Spirit that resurrects – makes alive (*Ephesians 2.1*).

What all of this boils down to is the matter of recognition. True, the five foolish had insufficient oil and were looking to buy some when the Bridegroom came, left, and shut the door. The grace of God that brings salvation has appeared to all but the fact of the appearance is not enough (*Titus 2.11*); neither is it enough to simply believe all the facts. (*James 2.19*)

In the final analysis, one must know Jesus Christ and be known by Him (*John 9.31*). After the wedding, the bridegroom appeared to the foolish virgins and said, *"I know you not."* The word *know* (**eido**) is a word that indicates perception because of a relationship. In order for someone to enter at the door and attend the marriage of the Lamb, that person must have a personal, working relationship with the Bridegroom. The oil of the Holy Spirit is vital to being allowed entrance, but it also serves to seal (*Ephesians 1.13; 4.30*) the personal relationship with recognition between the Bridegroom and the virgins. Personal recognition by the Bridegroom is paramount.

Knowing about Him is not enough. Knowing and believing about Him is not enough. Salvation involves a personal walk with the Savior. The fact that someone went down an aisle, cried, prayed, and felt good is not sufficient for admittance into eternity with Christ. Each person expecting admittance by the Bridegroom must be *in Christ* (*II Corinthians 5.17*).

If you do not have a personal relationship and walk with Christ, delay no longer. Make Jesus the Lord of your life and begin that wonderful experience of fellowship He offers to you as His personal gift.

The CSA Hunley and God's Word, II Timothy 2.19; Hebrews 6.19; I Peter 1.23

"Nevertheless the foundation of God standeth sure, having this seal, The Lord knoweth them that are his. And, Let every one that nameth the name of Christ depart from iniquity." (II Timothy 2.19)

In the early 1860's, toward the end of the War Between the States, Southern engineers and visionaries became desperate to find ways to break through the blockade in Charleston Harbor, SC. They had tried underwater mines (called torpedoes) designed to explode on contact with a ship's hull. There were also sunken mines that could be exploded electrically from shore when a ship passed over them (a brilliant idea that never quite seemed to work).

Another idea was called "torpedo boats" that were powered by steam and could move quietly in the water, and, with a long spar on the front laden with explosives, could ram an enemy ship from below the water line. This was an exciting idea, but even though these torpedo boats were small, they still could be seen and often stopped before doing any damage. Total surprise was impossible, so this never became the hoped-for super weapon of the Confederacy that would help end the blockade and ultimately end the war.

If the "spar-boat" with the torpedo ram protruding from the front was not the answer, maybe a Confederate submarine would work. This secret weapon named the *Hunley* is a story shrouded by mystery, tragedy, and courage. No one knows for certain how many attempts were made, now many crews died, and how many times it sank before it successfully sank the *USS Housatonic*, a part of the blockade in the Charleston Harbor.

Until the mid 1990s, when the *Hunley* was found almost buried in the soft mud on the floor of the river, much speculation had been made about its design and operation. It was a mystery because various people (experts) gave their theories concerning the methods of riveting and joining the boiler plates to ensure a water-tight seal. Others were asked to speculate about the propulsion system, navigation, and steering. A replica of the *Hunley* can still be seen on display at the Charleston (SC) Museum.

It was disconcerting to some to realize that after less than one hundred fifty years, there were neither definite designs nor written specifications for the small submarine. But, as we know from evolutionary theories, facts are not as important as answering questions using "creative imagination." Less than one hundred fifty years had passed between the *Hunley's* sinking and its resurrection, but the original proved to be genius beyond the guessers' expectations.

Although I am not qualified to speak with any real authority about the *Hunley*, and I know it raises excitement from some and disdain from others; I have seen it and have asked questions that have given me amazing answers. I would encourage you to check behind me and see for yourself.

The replica in Charleston resembles the *Hunley* mostly in size and appearance, but not in design. The method for joining the metal in the *Hunley* was years ahead of its time. Critics said that the Southern engineers could not have possibly used such advanced methods. They said, too, that the shaft which drove the propeller was attached directly when in reality it was introduced into a gear box that changed the gear ratio making it a more efficient craft. These are just two of the many bits of "misinformation" believed to be true of the *Hunley* until the *Hunley* itself proved the historians wrong.

It took less than one hundred fifty years for this bit of history to become corrupted into something that proves history to be less than perfectly credible. Think of all the misinformation passed along since the Middle Ages or before that. How reliable are the "experts" who teach us of the past?

Most of what we know of the Caesars comes from writings of which only a few copies remain and those were written hundreds or years after the fact and then from stories handed down by word of mouth. In the parlor game *"Gossip"* it seems quite impossible to pass one sentence through a group without the original having become totally corrupted. How much more difficult, could we presume, it is to maintain purity of fact through the tales of history?

Our text verse says that the saved are *". . . born again, not of corruptible seed, but of incorruptible, by the Word of God; which liveth and abideth forever."* (I Peter 1.23) Jesus Himself said, *"Till heaven and earth pass, one jot or one tittle shall in no wise pass from the law, till all be fulfilled."* (Matthew 5.18)

Some have suggested a problem with the thousands of copies of God's Word extant today. What is so amazing is that, of all the extant manuscripts, relatively few discrepancies are apparent and none significantly change the fundamentals of the faith. This fact alone should add weight to the accuracy of God's Word as well as to God's ability to preserve it.

What is more amazing than the accuracy and agreement between the various manuscripts and how they give weight to each other is the fact that people would more readily believe documents written hundreds of years after an event, knowing the possibility of human error and personal interpretation, than to believe the Bible that has never been proven to contain any error at all. Nearly 2,000 years have come and gone since our Lord walked on this earth; and the writers wrote their accounts no more than forty years after (most within a few years) the events. Copies of these writings have been dated to within ten years of the close of the canon of Scripture. Thousands of these copies are in existence and ones found recently verify the accuracy of the ones from which our Bibles have been translated. The veracity and accuracy of God's Word cannot be denied.

Remember the *Hunley*? Of all the possible accounts from relatives and friends, not more than three or four generations removed, no one seemed able to build a viable and accurate replica. Granted, this project was completed in secret and the acts that make up Holy Scripture were done in the open, but still there are skeptics about the truth of God's Word and apparently none who had taken issue with the *Hunley's* design.

In addition to that is the fact of an omnipotent God Who settled His Word forever. Just as He was able, through His Holy Spirit, to inspire the Bible, so He is able to preserve His Word throughout the many years. When conflicts and contradictions appear, our best Rock upon which to stand and build is still God's Word. *"Yea, let God be true, but every man a liar."* (Romans 3.4)

The Whole Man, Ecclesiastes 12.13, 14

"Let us hear the conclusion of the whole matter: Fear God, and keep his commandments: for this *is* the whole *duty* of man. For God shall bring every work into judgment, with every secret thing, whether *it be* good, or whether *it be* evil." (Ecclesiastes 12.13, 14)

Some years ago I heard a well-known preacher bring a message from this passage. He stressed the idea of man's duty in keeping God's commandments and that, along with fearing God; were the two factors making up the responsible duty of man toward God.

By examining *Ecclesiastes 12.13* carefully, one will find, in the King James Version of the Bible, the word *"duty"* is given in italics. That suggests *"duty"* was added by the translators to help the translation make sense and read smoothly. It is quite proper and does suggest duty as a part of the godly man, but the emphasis should be placed on what makes up the whole man – not just his duty.

In order to get the complete picture we must understand some of Solomon's journey as he comes to this conclusion. He begins his book by identifying himself as the *"Preacher" (Ecclesiastes 1.1)*. Differing from our modern concept of a preacher, here the preacher is a gatherer of information, insights, sayings, and wisdom rather than someone who stands behind a pulpit proclaiming God's truth. This preacher sets out to gather information empirically through observation, testimony, eye-witness accounts, and experimentation. Through this process he attempts to prove his hypothesis – *". . . vanity of vanities, all is vanity." (**hebel** – "vanity, emptiness, meaninglessness")*.

He tries various postulates and suppositions so that his words (*verse 1*, **dabar** – *"words, speech, matter"*), his database of information, will carry weight with the hearers. When he comes to his conclusion at the end of his work (*Ecclesiastes 12.13*), his stated observations are quite pointed, frank, and terse.

After all of his personal research, he comes to the same conclusion – all that the world offers is meaningless action and reaction. His view had not changed, but his depth of wisdom had.

Ecclesiastes 12.9 begins with the word *"moreover,"* which suggests the preacher had added much wisdom to his knowledge through his pursuits. Through this newly acquired wisdom, the preacher taught (drilled) the people with knowledge.

His teachings did, indeed, carry weight as he gave good advice through his many proverbs. He set in order the facts and truth in ways that delighted (*acceptable – **hepes** – "delight, pleasure, desire"*) the listeners. He used a method of teaching that is still effective today – goads and nails.

A goad is a long, pointed stick used to move idle animals in a desired direction. Modern goads (often called "hot-shots") are used around stockyards to move cattle along to the auction floor. Once, while visiting a stockyard with my father-in-law, a handler, who was working with a particularly ornery Brahma bull, applied the "hot-shot" to the bull's backside to encourage him along. When the 20,000 volts were applied, the bull not only began moving, but also jumped a six-foot high restraining wall. The goad did not force the bull to move, but it made him want to do so.

After helping the lethargic hearer with goads, the preacher proceeded to give truths that can make solid what has been taught – hence, the nails. Nails are used to make things permanent. His desire was to bring his hearers to the same conclusion which he had discovered.

Verse 12 suggests that wisdom and the perfection of the individual are not found in books or in much study (*poring over information to the point of exhaustion*), but in finding a purpose for the matter (*"information," see II Timothy 3.7*).

His conclusion includes three main points. The first is man's responsibility to fear God. Fearing God is not only the beginning of knowledge (*Proverbs 1.7*), but also the beginning of wisdom (*Proverbs 9.10*). All information must be filtered through the truth of God's Word. To fear God we must consider Him more important than anything else in our lives.

The second responsibility is to keep God's commandments. The word *"keep"* carries the idea of *"guarding and protecting"* more than doing something. In all of his learning, Solomon came to the conclusion that more of what man is may be found in who he is rather than what he does.

In considering the whole man, Solomon urges his hearers to go beyond the immediate by remembering there will be a day of judgment (*verse 14, see also II Corinthians 5.10*).

The whole man should be consumed with his relationship with God. More than duty is the personal awareness that all in the world is passing, but God is forever. So then, the whole man is responsible to guard God's holiness and to keep himself in a proper relationship with the only One who matters.

Why did Jesus cry? John 11.35

"Jesus wept." (John 11.35)

At first glance, this story seems simple enough. Lazarus was dead and in the grave. He died four days prior *(John 11.17, 39)* and had begun decaying. There was no doubt of this fact because after Jesus had tried to lessen the pain of the loss for the disciples by using the metaphor of sleep *(John 11.11)*, He flatly said, *"Lazarus is dead." (John 11.14)*.

When I think of this verse, my heart revels in the humanity of Jesus. Just think – God became flesh, dwelled among us, and experienced our pain. This is one angle from which to view this scene. As a matter of record, many godly men hold to this position exclusively – that Jesus grieved along with the other mourners over the physical loss of Lazarus who was obviously a real friend.

At least one objection to this view stands in the way. Not only did Jesus know, personally and vividly, that He would see Lazarus in the resurrection *(John 11.25, 26)*, but also, the reunion would be soon (Jesus was crucified only a few days later.). Jesus, Who as God knew all things, would only be relieved that His friend had preceded Him into glory.

Another thought we should consider is the idea that Jesus wept because of the people's unbelief. Actually this position is held by a majority of commentators (at least a majority of the ones I have studied). This thought gain's credibility because of Jesus' reaction in verse 38 to their questions in verse 37.

"And some of them said, Could not this man, which opened the eyes of the blind, have caused that even this man should not have died." (John 11.37) The questions were valid and it shows that the askers did believe in Jesus to some degree – just not for complete salvation. Jesus, however, did not answer, but *"groaned"* (**embrimaomai** – *"to be greatly moved or agitated"*) in Himself *(John 11.38)*. To some, this groaning indicates Jesus' deep grief over their lack of belief in Him as the Messiah.

This groaning, however, is the second time Jesus groaned – the first is recorded in verse 33 after Mary chided Him for His tardiness in responding to their summons. *"Lord, if thou hast been here, my brother had not died."* Here Scripture records that Jesus groaned and *"troubled"* (**tarasso** – *"to stir up, to trouble, to agitate"*) Himself (**heautou** – reflexive pronoun *"himself"*).

Putting these two thoughts together brings us to a third possibility – stress. Not many hold to this view, but someone in my junior high Bible class suggested it; and it does seem to include all the elements. Stress, though, does not seem to cover the fact that Jesus stayed longer than He needed to stay. Although according to Jewish custom a person must be dead for at least three days before he could be legally pronounced dead, Jesus could have hurried and stopped all the grieving and put His stress to rest.

So then, why did Jesus weep and why did He groan?

Throughout Jesus' life, situations arose in which Jesus proved Himself by His actions and miracles. Even though people recognized His "difference," most needed signs or miracles before they would believe Him to be Messiah. At times, Jesus seemed to hesitate prior to the occurrence of some great events.

Jesus, the perfect human and God, always did His Father's bidding; but, on occasion, He sought His Father's approval and reassurance. When in the garden, His prayer was *"O my Father, if it be possible, let this cup pass from me: nevertheless, not as I will, but as thou wilt."* *(Matthew 26.39b, see verse 42).* During this time of prayer, His agony and grief was so great that He *"sweat . . . as it were great drops of blood."* *(Luke 22.44)*

All of these events were determined by the Triune God prior to creation and were included in His plan for man's salvation. These plans included the death and resurrection of Lazarus. To the believing Lazarus, death was a greater blessing than resurrection *(Psalm 116.15).*

Since Jesus knew of the agonies of this life and the manifold blessings enjoyed in God's presence, He would sorrow and grieve over the thought of bringing His friend back to life. Jesus knew the religious leaders would seek to kill Lazarus and others would hound him – making his life miserable. Jesus also knew that Lazarus would eventually taste the bitter cup of death again.

Jesus did not weep because of personal grief or because of stress (although these emotions may have been present). The groaning which caused Jesus to weep may have been due to unbelief; but only indirectly. What seems more probable is that Jesus groaned and wept because He knew how Lazarus was enjoying his "afterlife" experience and would loathe coming back.

By the way, it is interesting that Lazarus never remarks of his experience even though he later sits at a meal with his family and friends (*John 12.1, 2*). Maybe he was angry. Maybe he was sad. Maybe he had nothing to say. Or maybe his mind was so in a different place that he simply longed to be there. But that is a subject for another time.

www.ingramcontent.com/pod-product-compliance
Lightning Source LLC
Chambersburg PA
CBHW052008090426
42741CB00008B/1605

9 781257 090389